LUNATIC

andrew fraser

LUNATIC SOUP

Hardie Grant Books

Published in 2008
Hardie Grant Books
85 High Street
Prahran, Victoria 3181, Australia
www.hardiegrant.com.au

Cataloguing-in-Publication data is available from
the National Library of Australia.

Fraser, Andrew Roderick.
Lunatic soup : inside the madness of maximum security / Andrew Fraser.
   978 1 7406 6629 9
   Fraser, Andrew Roderick.
   Lawyers – Australia – Biography.
   Prisoners – Australia – Biography.
   Prisons – Australia.
   Serial murderers – Australia.
340.092

Edited by Sally Moss
Cover design by Pat Sofra
Cover photograph by Lindy Allen
Typeset in Goudy Old Style by Kirby Jones
Printed and bound in Australia by Trojan Press

10 9 8 7 6 5 4 3 2 1

Thanks to Victor the journey
has just begun.

Contents

Acknowledgements

Thanks to John Sylvester and Andrew Rule authors of the Underbelly series for their assistance with background material.

Preface

By the time you read this book I will have been out of jail for more than two years and the odyssey that began with my arrest on 13 September 1999 will have concluded. My two-year parole will at long last have ground to a useless conclusion and after more than nine years I will again be a truly free man, no longer subject to any vagaries or constraints of the Victorian Government. It has been a long haul.

My original intention after release was to work on a mate's farm for some of the time and rebuild my shattered life, spending time with my children, for the remainder. But once I agreed to give evidence against Peter Dupas any thoughts of a quiet life went right out the window. I had no intention of writing a book about my experiences until the publisher Sandy Grant talked me into meeting with him, and at the end of that meeting I had been convinced to write not just one book but at least two books.

My first effort, *Court in the Middle*, was released in 2007. It was relatively easy for me to write because, among the trials and tribulations, many of the episodes I recalled were pleasant experiences in an interesting life.

This second book, however, has been no such animal. In writing it, I have had to take myself back to extremely unpleasant and sometimes dark and scary times and places,

places I would have preferred not to revisit. Delving back into the dark recesses of my mind to life in Sirius East, the maximum security division at Port Phillip Prison, was extremely difficult. I struggled with a lot of the content as I often found it distressing to write about.

In this book, as in the previous one, I am critical of the legal system as we know it, the appalling state of prisons and the disgraceful way in which consecutive governments have played the Law and Order card only for their own short-term (political) benefit and not for anybody else's.

As long as there is no rehabilitation in jail (and it is not a question of degree; there is none) then society will continue to suffer. The penal system will continue releasing back into that society people who have done nothing during their prison system but sit on their bums and learn from fellow inmates the nuances of committing further and more complex crimes. Each time one of these former prisoners reoffends, society as a whole becomes a victim of crime.

Needless to say, I have been most interested in the reaction to *Court in the Middle* by politicians, the police, the courts and those who administer the prison system – namely, the Corrections Commissioner and all his employees. Not one of these people has had a single thing to say publicly about my book. No one has claimed that anything in it is inaccurate, incorrect or a lie. What have they all done instead? The usual trick: stick your head in the sand, ignore the elephant in the room, and hope to Christ that Andrew Fraser will go away. I won't!

As you read this book you will note that my contempt for the disgraceful state of the system has not diminished. I intend to keep agitating for prison and drug reform until somebody takes notice and the powers that be are faced with the inevitable: they have to address these issues head-on, no more prevarication.

I am in the unique position of being able to assess and make my observations from three perspectives: that of a practising criminal lawyer who visited nearly every jail in this country in the course of his professional life, that of an inmate, and finally that of a pivotal Crown witness.

As a lawyer you think you know and understand the system. But believe me, when the door slams shut on you personally for the first time, you are in another world. You are completely at the mercy of the whims and prejudices of those who run the system and hence rule your life inside. There is nothing you can do about it because the Court of Criminal Appeal in Victoria has effectively washed its hands of administering the criminal justice system within the prisons. The Court of Criminal Appeal has stated that proposition on more than one occasion. "We cannot tell the prison authorities how to run a prison," is what you will hear them say. Pontius Pilate is alive and well and living in William Street, Melbourne. This leaves one wondering what hope is available to any prisoner who has been wrongly done by. I give a classic example of this later in the book.

LUNATIC SOUP

After reading *Court in the Middle* some people said to me: "How did you get through it all? I don't think I would have made it." In reply I ask another question: How do you deal with any crisis that life may dish up to you? It need not be the trauma of a prison cell. Anything can happen to any of us; for instance, the death of a child (every parent's worst fear), ill health, serious injury, loss of a business, going broke … the list is endless. There is only one answer: Face the music! Place one foot in front of the other, never wavering in your resolve to somehow get through to the other end of the disaster that your life has become. One foot in front of the other, and days turn into weeks, weeks into months. Then, after what feels like an eternity, one year has elapsed, then another. Finally the big day arrives: you have made it, you are going home! Before that, however, you have to do a lot of soul searching and be brutally honest with yourself; otherwise you are wasting your time and the only person you are cheating with your delusional behaviour is yourself. You walk very carefully and do not rush in where angels fear to tread because to do so could well bring you unstuck.

Life is the ultimate teacher and there is so much to learn. As long as we learn from our mistakes then it has all been worth the pain and misery that these traumas bring. Life is great. I hope you enjoy *Lunatic Soup*.

Andrew Fraser
Melbourne, 2008

Chapter 1
Muster Up!

Nervous, very, very dreadfully nervous I had been
and am; but why WILL you say I am mad? The
disease had sharpened my senses, not destroyed, not
dulled them. Above all was the sense of hearing acute.
I heard all things in the heaven and in the earth. I
heard many things in hell. How, then, am I mad?
Hearken! and observe how heathily, how calmly, I
can tell you the whole story.

– EDGAR ALLAN POE, *THE TELL-TALE HEART*

Muster up! Muster up! Stand by your open cell doors for count. Muster up. No drinking. No talking. No smoking. No farting (ha ha). Stand by your open cell doors for count.

Sirius East unit at Port Phillip Prison, one of Victoria's two maximum security prisons. Here I am, placed in "protection from protection" along with thirty-seven of this state's worst criminals, a number of whom have committed crimes so heinous that the perpetrators are never to be released. Protection from protection means blokes who need general protection in jail and blokes from whom the rest of the jail needs protection from.

How did I come to be here? Well may you ask! Unfortunately the answer is simplicity itself. As a lawyer of twenty-eight years' standing I had worked hard to build a successful practice. I practised criminal law and was available to appear for people seven days a week, twenty-four hours a day. During that time, needless to say, I made many enemies in the police force. But none more markedly than the now disbanded Drug Squad, and in particular Detective Senior Sergeant Wayne Strawhorn. While I have now been released for nearly two years, Mr Strawhorn has only just recently had his appeal against conviction and sentence dismissed for the corrupt activities of selling methylamphetamine precursor chemicals to Lewis Moran, a now-deceased client of mine, and his son Mark Moran. These men's deaths came about during Melbourne's notorious underworld war of the late 1990s and early 2000s.

When I realised Strawhorn was corrupt I took a large body of information regarding his activities to the National Crime Authority. Little did I know that to talk to the NCA was to set in motion my own demise.

To understand the full story we need to go back a few years, to when I first took cocaine in a social setting.

Anyone who says they don't like cocaine has, in my view, never tried it. Cocaine is a drug that seduces and destroys. It is all consuming. For many years I limited my cocaine use to the social level. It was only when I met Carl Urbanec, Werner Roberts, and Roberts's wife Andrea Mohr that the wheels started to fall off my life. These three people, eventually my co-accused, were professional cocaine traffickers and importers around the world, and had been for many years.

I had acted on behalf of Werner Roberts in relation to a back injury claim. Upon settlement of the claim I agreed to meet Werner for a drink at a bar in St Kilda, where I used to live, so that he could pay me for those legal services. After a couple of glasses of wine he asked "Do you still like a snort"? – indicating that he knew I didn't mind using cocaine. I told him I did indeed like a snort. He suggested I follow him to his home as he had a present for me. I followed him and there he presented me with a large lump – approximately a quarter of an ounce – of extremely high quality cocaine. The drug was suddenly readily available and literally around the corner from where I lived.

While I was acquiring for myself a nice little habit I foolishly went to the National Crime Authority to discuss Mr Strawhorn's corrupt activities. The police officer I spoke to at the National Crime Authority was clearly corrupt himself as he then referred this matter directly to the Drug Squad. In other words, he told Strawhorn that I was onto him for his corrupt activities. By having a substantial cocaine habit, I stupidly gave Strawhorn my head on a plate. My whole world came crashing down. The problem with cocaine use is that it makes you feel that anything is possible; it makes you feel ten feet tall and bullet proof!

In a few short months I grabbed everything I had worked my entire adult life to achieve and tossed it all away in a drug-addled binge that landed me in the go-slow for a long time. It has not been lost on me, in the many years that I have had to ponder my fate since my arrest, how true it is that you can take many, many years to establish yourself but it only takes a short period of idiocy to come unstuck. This is precisely what happened to me and I have only myself to blame.

I ended up in the dock of the County Court in Melbourne where I pleaded Guilty to a charge of being knowingly concerned with the importation of a commercial quantity of cocaine. The judge showed me no mercy, notwithstanding the fact that I was fifty years of age, a father of two young children and without previous convictions and that I had been a lawyer my entire adult life. I received a crushing sentence of seven years with a minimum of five years to serve before being eligible for release on parole. All the lawyers advising me had suggested that, if I pleaded guilty, my sentence should be around six to twelve months. Even the Crown prosecutor told my counsel that the Crown would not appeal a twelve-month sentence.

Mr Strawhorn was still at the top of his game and, notwithstanding his corrupt activities, made sure that my life was in danger when I went to jail. Rather than being

sent to a prison farm up the bush, as is usual in cases such as
mine because I was not a risk of reoffending and I was
certainly not a risk of running away, I was sent to Sirius East
at Port Phillip, the worst of the worst. There I was chucked
into a unit full of psychopaths and madmen who were likely
to do anything at any time and often did. How the coppers
must have chuckled with glee at the prospect of the rough
ride they anticipated I would have!

Looking back now, the irony of all this is clear. While in
Sirius East I met Peter Dupas, a notorious serial killer and
mutilator of defenceless women. As the cards fell, after my
release I was to give evidence against Dupas as Crown
witness and it was my evidence that was pivotal to the
prosecution case and helped secure his conviction.

Here I am, still shell-shocked at where I have ended up,
standing by my open cell door for my first muster with my
new cell mate, one Andrew Davies, a serial paedophile who,
upon conviction for the offences for which he was then in
jail, received no minimum sentence – which means he was
never to be released. Luckily for him, on an appeal he
received a minimum term of fourteen years for his horrific
offences, which I will come to later.

Before muster, I was taken from the Melbourne Remand
Prison in shackles (a humiliating experience indeed) and
was unceremoniously chucked into a cell with this person.
For somebody like me, who had acted for crooks all my adult

life and had been in and out of probably every jail in this country as a professional visitor, it was a rude shock to be sharing accommodation with somebody like this. Paedophiles were the only category of offender that I actively avoided acting for as a lawyer. This particular cell had been converted from a single cell to a "two outer" – jail slang for a shared cell – and was filthy.

As the door was slammed shut on me by the screws (the prison officers even refer to themselves as "screws") I stood wondering what would happen next. It was then that I was first hit by the all-pervading stench that I will take with me to my grave. It was a mixture of stale White Ox roll-your-own tobacco, stale unwashed male body and clothing, cheap disinfectant and stale semen. It turns out that Davies was a serial masturbator and frankly didn't care if I was in the cell or not when he indulged himself. This man's IQ would just make room temperature and on any assessment he was bereft of all human dignity. His entire existence revolved around Commodore motor cars and scavenging discarded cigarette butts from rubbish bins around the jail and then re-rolling them into cigarettes to smoke. Never having smoked myself, I find cigarette smoke offensive at the best of times, but being stuck in a cell with this bloke who habitually rolled cigarettes out of other people's butts and then smoked them nearly drove me to distraction. In the end I had to threaten him physically that if he didn't stop smoking in the cell there would be trouble.

At this particular time Davies was in custody for the abduction and digital rape of two young girls aged six at Nagambie in country Victoria. At this time my son was ten and my daughter was eight years old. The very thought of being cooped up with somebody such as this revolted me. But there was no point in asking for a relocation. One screw in particular, when asked any question, delighted in standing up and grabbing himself by the crutch and yelling at the top of his voice: "Suck my big fat one!" End of discussion! Makes asking for anything rather pointless, doesn't it?

When I was first banged up with Davies he refused to acknowledge that he had ever been in trouble. He merely stated that he'd been wrongly charged with the current offences, that he was not guilty and that he had been illegally refused bail in relation to these charges. Well, that turned out to be complete and utter rubbish. Having checked out his criminal history since, it seems to have started in about 1993 when he had raped a seven-year-old girl in a toilet block only one day after being given an intensive corrections order for another crime against a child and while serving that community-based order.

A couple of weeks later, and then again in 1998, Davies was found inside a school toilet block. He was given community-based orders in relation to all of these charges, judgements that allow criminals to serve a sentence while remaining on the street. It is unbelievable that he was given such sentences because the significant aspect of all his offending is that he refused to partake in any sex offenders' programs. How in heaven's name can the Corrections Commissioner, the Office of Corrections, the courts and the Parole Board allow these sorts of people on the street if they refuse to undergo sex offenders' programs?

Towards the end of my sentence I was at Fulham Prison with another rapist by the name of David Lakeman and he refused parole – that is, to be released early –because it would require him to undergo a sex offenders' program. Instead he served his parole period in jail, the logic being that once he had completed his full sentence he would not be subject to any sex offenders' programs. It came to pass and he was allowed out the door without the Parole Board having any hold over him at all. This is an outrageous situation and society should be rightly outraged. Once again this man maintained throughout the entirety of his sentence that he was wrongly charged and convicted and was not guilty. Does anyone notice a pattern emerging with these blokes?

Davies asked me to read his brief, which I did because I was new in jail, didn't know the ropes and was frankly scared stiff. I was revolted by the brief and the statements of the two young girls. Davies was clearly identified by them because he looks somewhat like a chimpanzee and that's precisely how they described him. He said that it was all bullshit and that it wasn't him, he had been wrongly charged, he'd been singled out for special treatment by the coppers – blah, blah, blah.

Having acted for a number of sex offenders over many years, I've noticed one common thread running through all their offences, and that is a complete denial of any wrongdoing, even after conviction and imposition of a prison sentence.

A classic example of such a mindset was many years ago when a young bloke was referred to me by the senior partner of one of Australia's more prestigious law firms. The senior partner rang me, introduced himself and said that a dear old friend of his had a son who had got himself into a little trouble. I asked what sort of trouble. He said that the son was a scout master, to which I replied "How many scouts have complained?" He was surprised that I had hit the nail on the head.

A couple of the scouts had made a complaint about sexual assaults by the scout master. The young man attended my office and sat down. He was incensed that he had been charged and strident in proclaiming his innocence. He explained to me that he and another scout master had taken a large number of scouts away for the weekend. When they arrived at the camping ground it was raining so heavily that they only had time to put up two tents, not all of the tents that were required, and as a result the accommodation in the tents was very, very tight and, guess what, when he woke up the next morning he had a scout's penis in his mouth!

This is a true story and this was put to me in deadly seriousness. I sat there in my office absolutely dumbfounded that anybody would think that any court or jury on this planet would be stupid enough to accept that fiction as a defence. It was all I could do not to burst out laughing at the absurdity of it all. I told the young bloke that he would have noticed that I hadn't made one note during the interview and that if he thought I was going to court to run that defence for him he'd better think again.

He went away and came back with his parents, who were equally outraged at his having being charged. I had to give them the bad news in words of one syllable so that there was no misunderstanding, and he ended up pleading Guilty. He got a short jail sentence, as he should.

Davies, likewise, was adamant that he was not guilty, so much so that he then pleaded Not Guilty, went to trial and, surprise!, was convicted. He was then sentenced by his Honour Judge Bill White in the County Court at Melbourne to an indefinite term because it was clear that this man refused to accept responsibility for his actions and that the prospect of any meaningful rehabilitation was negligible. Unfortunately, on appeal, that indefinite term of imprisonment was reduced to sixteen years with a minimum of fourteen before Davies was eligible for parole. Having lived in the same cell with Davies for a few months, it was apparent to me that he had absolutely no intention of ever changing, because you can't change until you come to terms with and admit your own transgressions.

Polonius, in Shakespeare's play *Hamlet*, said "This above all: to thine own self be true." This is the key to not reoffending. This man will be released and will reoffend. The logic from the Court of Appeal was that he will be in jail for such a long while that he well may think about taking sex offenders' counselling while in jail. In my view the chances of that happening are a million to one and drifting. Davies had a record of twenty-nine prior offences, which included offences against three small children. I believe people with this sort of background do not deserve to live in our society again. Davies was in protection because in jail paedophiles (known as rock spiders because they can creep into very small crevices) are despised by the mainstream prison population. He would in all likelihood have been killed by other inmates in mainstream. The incomprehensible part was that I was in protection with him!

It was interesting to note, however, that rapist/murderers such as Peter Dupas or Raymond Edmonds were not in the same danger within Sirius East because their offences weren't considered by inmates to be as bad as those against children. Work that one out for yourself!

The only thing I saw Davies do to fill his day while I was living with him was to work on nuts and bolts, which is the rehabilitation all inmates receive in jail. The work involved the assembly of a bolt with a sleeve and a nut, known by the trade name of Dynabolt. You take the bolt, you put the sleeve on, screw on the nut and throw the Dynabolt in a tub. Try doing that for hours per day without going nuts yourself. The other thing Davies did was take all the drugs prescribed for him, and they must have been substantial because he would be lucky to get past eight o'clock at night without becoming comatose. That is how people are treated in jail. Not once while I was in protection, which was fifteen months, did I see Davies speak to a counsellor or a psychologist about his problems, even after he had been convicted for the umpteenth time.

The first thing you notice about jail is the complete futility of it all. Despair is all too common and some blokes opt out permanently. The rest of us are left to "kick along with it", as they say in jail. It was during this period that depression and panic attacks first became known to me. All my life I have had been a bit of an optimist, with the view that the glass is half full rather than half empty, and depression hit hard. The panic attacks are the worst: an attack often hits as you lie awake in the middle of the night. You say to yourself that there is logically nothing to worry about, there is no reason to panic, yet it still goes on and you have to hang in there and sit it out.

So here I stand completely bewildered, terrified. I'm like a rabbit caught in the headlights. I don't know what's going to happen here but this place is full of mad and bad bastards and anything could happen to me. I hold very real fears for my safety.

I look around the cell block and try to get a grasp on who's who at the zoo.

Chapter 2

Who's Who at the Zoo

*It is not usually considered a sign of robust mental
health to be hearing voices from burning bushes.*

– ROBERT SOPALSKY, *JUNK FOOD MONKEYS*

I cast my eye around the unit. I recognise a number of faces I
have only ever read about. Some of the state's most infamous
rapists, murderers and child molesters are in this unit. What
have I done to deserve this? I am a middle-aged ex-lawyer
who had a´raging cocaine habit, no dishonesty or violence.
If I am going to get through this I am going to have to play
my cards very carefully.

Not only am I banged up with Andrew Davies; I look
straight across from me and there is Leslie Camilleri, the
infamous Bega-schoolgirl murderer. Camilleri, while on an
amphetamine-fuelled binge that went for some days,
abducted, raped and murdered two schoolgirls, Lauren Barry,

aged fourteen, and Nicole Collins, sixteen, who were hitchhiking home from school. Camilleri and a co-offender who gave evidence against Camilleri took the girls, held them hostage for days and tortured them. Camilleri and his co-accused Lindsay Beckett ultimately killed them. He was sentenced by His Honour Mr Justice Vincent to life with no minimum – that is, never to be released.

For some reason, when I first met Camilleri in Sirius East, he immediately took a dislike to me. I did not know the bloke from a bar of soap and had never met him. The very next morning he walked up to me at the nuts and bolts table, chested me and said "You're a cunt and I'm fucking well going to kill you." Here we go. Day one and I have already copped a death threat – terrific! Welcome to the nick!

At first I found this comment somewhat off-putting, but I soon realised just what sort of bloke Camilleri was. He is a big man, but unfortunately for him he has a brain and a heart the size of a split pea. Every night Camilleri thought it was hilarious to fart on muster. Of course, that means everyone has to wait until muster is completed without being interrupted. He is dumb, stupid, and petulant and is prone to throw what you would describe, if he was a child, as a tantrum. The difference is that, with a child, you tell them to get on with it. In jail Camilleri throws a tantrum and everyone runs around trying to calm him down. The whole performance is attention seeking. Personally, if he threatened to neck himself in front of me I would give him the rope.

The reason for the panic by the screws is the amount of paperwork they need to complete if there is a death in custody, and work is the natural enemy of screws! They may also have to answer a lot of awkward questions when the coppers investigate these deaths.

Camilleri was a keen painter and whenever he spat the dummy, the first thing he did, in an act of petulance, was to throw all his paints in the rubbish bin. Given that nobody ever visits this man and he has no money apart from what he earns in jail, to throw away his paints like that was a huge statement but it also indicated that the bloke was an idiot who didn't think things through. That's probably what landed him in jail. Why anybody bothered to help to retrieve his paints, I do not know. But I soon saw that for all his bluff and bravado he had no dash at all. It was for that reason, and that reason alone, that he was only capable of torturing and killing defenceless young girls.

One day I did in fact see Camilleri have a go at a bloke out in the garden with the prison's pitchfork. He couldn't even do that properly and the other bloke, who was fairly handy with his fists, turned around and decked him. The screws did nothing about that. Nobody ever asked how this evil bloke got hold of the fork, which was supposed to have been under lock and key at the time.

After Camilleri threatened to knock me the first day in Sirius East I gave him a wide berth because, while I wasn't scared of him, he was unpredictable and therefore capable of the odd bit of rash behaviour. The only other time I had a problem with him was towards the end of my time in Sirius East when, just before the final muster for the day, he appeared at my cell door holding a jug of boiling water which, he announced, he was going to throw over me before killing me. This is a commonly used tactic in jail as the boiling water disorientates you and you are then defenceless against attack. On looking back now it is obvious to me that I had become a product of my environment and was usually hyper vigilant. People have made the observation that upon my release I was as jumpy as a jack rabbit, forever wary, whereas I thought that I was normal and coping with my release beautifully.

If I was vigilant, you might ask, why was I sitting with my cell door open? The answer is simple: it was the end of the day and all doors are to be open for lockdown muster. More importantly the lolly trolley (medication trolley) had been, and by this time all and sundry (with the exception of my good self) were usually knocked rotten by their medication and were out like lights in their caves.

Camilleri was one very enthusiastic lolly consumer but for reasons unknown on this night he was still up and very much about! I was sitting reading (as per usual) in my cell. Here we go, young Fraser, time to stand up and be counted! Camilleri made one mistake: I saw him hesitate, albeit momentarily. I jumped up, grabbed the plastic barbecue chair I was sitting on and belted him as hard as I could over the head. He almost dissolved before my eyes and he bolted. The screws could not have missed this incident, yet nothing was ever said to me about it.

I should at this stage indicate how muster is conducted. Although this is the age of the microchip, and we have sent people into space, muster is still carried out with a muster sheet. This is the system that was used on the First Fleet when convicts were first sent to this country. Two hundred plus years later the same system is still being used. Two screws walk past each cell, one with the muster sheet, to record the number of prisoners in the cell. When they come to a single cell, the other officer looks in and says "one", then the officer with the muster sheet marks that cell off as having one person in it; at a double cell the officer says "two", and two are marked off. You have no idea how often the count is incorrect, meaning that the prison officers who mustered my unit, Sirius East, with a maximum of thirty-eight men in it, could not count to thirty-eight correctly, believe it or not. When the count is not correct there is a recount, which, more often than not, is again incorrect. They then have what's called a lockdown count. A lockdown count means every prisoner throughout the entire jail is locked in his cell and then counted in situ. If that is not correct, they do it all again. When the count is finally correct, the number of prisoners in each unit is rung in to the nerve centre of the jail (and I use that term advisedly) where some genius adds up the numbers in all of the units and often also comes to the wrong answer. Given that Port Phillip is a jail of over 700 prisoners, it is incredible to think that muster is not done electronically.

In the cell opposite Camilleri was his arch nemesis, Peter Dupas. When I first met Dupas he was serving life with no minimum for the murder of Nicole Patterson, his treating psychologist. He has since been convicted of two more murders, which I will deal with in greater detail later.

Next door to Dupas was Raymond Edmunds, the infamous Mr Stinky. Edmunds is a great mate of Dupas and they formed the basis of one of the "crews" (in jail gangs are called crews) that ran Sirius East. He is now an old man, fat, no hair, no teeth, in poor health but with an amicable disposition: apparently the complete antithesis of the monster he clearly was when he murdered the teenagers Abina Madill and Garry Heywood in 1966. For those offences Edmunds was sentenced to life without a minimum sentence being set. At the time, that was the only option available to a sentencing court for murder, but during the course of Edmunds's imprisonment, the legislation was changed and a number of crooks had made applications for minimum sentences and had been successful.

It was an eye opener for me to meet this old man, who was repentant and remorseful, and try to create a mental picture of what he must have been like when younger and committing those horrendous offences. He asked me whether I thought he should apply for a fixed term. I said that, at that stage, having done well over twenty years in jail and given his age and his health, he would probably have at least some chance of receiving a fixed sentence. However, when I had this discussion with Edmunds I was not aware of the remainder of his past. It turns out he is suspected of at least thirty other rapes, including one where he threatened, and then raped, a woman in front of her five-year-old son. He was later convicted of three rapes and two attempted rapes. It was afterwards that he received the life sentence without a minimum. With new technology available police are investigating Edmunds for his involvement in other rapes and potentially other murders. Stay tuned.

Edmunds subsequently made an application to receive a fixed term but the Director of Public Prosecutions, being armed with all of the facts, opposed it. The application was refused by the Supreme Court and Edmunds will now never be released – he will die in jail, a general prospect that I personally have considered many times, both while in jail and after release. If I was in that position, bereft of hope, I think I would probably end it all. By contrast, Edmunds appears to be able to kick along with it. He still has the support of his family and does receive visits from them. One wonders what goes through his mind at night, in the long dark hours between lockdown and let-out the next morning, when a prisoner is very much alone with his thoughts. I sincerely hope that he regrets his behaviour to the day he dies, having brought so much pain and suffering to so many people.

I should also mention that prisoners who are serving life sentences with no minimum are not left in the one maximum security jail for their entire life. Every one or two years the authorities move them between Port Phillip Prison and Barwon Prison outside Geelong, which is the other maximum security jail in Victoria, to give them a bit of a change of scenery. These men, it must be borne in mind, will never, ever leave maximum security or protection. They cannot go into the mainstream because of their crimes and they will never be removed to a prison farm. Their whole existence is spent in maximum security under the very strict regimes that apply. Considering the total lack of rehabilitation, or effectively anything to stimulate them or educate the prisoners, is it any wonder that the existing jail politics often blow over into violence, usually purely out of frustration and boredom?

Paul Gorman is a serial rapist who was quite unrepentant about his offending. He was one of Dupas's mates and also was part of the Dupas crew. They were the dominant crew in the unit and the other inmates were justifiably wary of them. When I met Gorman he had served about eleven years out of a thirteen year sentence in maximum security for rape. As I wrote in my previous book, not long after I had been placed in Sirius East, I was pacing up and down in the small exercise yard referred to as the "chook pen", wondering how in God's name I was ever going to get through my sentence. Gorman was sitting in the yard and said to me the only way that I would get through the sentence was to never have my mind outside the walls of the prison; my mind must be fixed inside the walls and I would get through it all.

In maximum security all you can see is barbed wire, concrete floors and concrete walls topped with razor wire. It is a mentally devastating sight. The desolation of it all presses in on you, every moment of every day. I looked at Gorman, who did not present a very palatable sight: he is overweight, doesn't wear his false teeth, does no exercise and does nothing constructive with his day except smoke cigarettes and play billiards. When he is released into the community, having done his thirteen years, he will have done absolutely nothing to improve himself.

I looked at Gorman and realised suddenly that had provided me with my first very important lesson in jail. What he had said was obviously incorrect, so for me to survive all I needed to do was the exact opposite of what he stated. Namely, the authorities may well have my body, but they would never have my mind, and from that moment forward I changed my attitude to serving the remainder of my sentence.

Every waking minute I spent pursuing matters that were on the outside. With the exception of crime reports (for obvious reasons), I read the newspapers from cover to cover each day, even the obituaries! I kept in contact with friends on the outside. I wrote letters and I received a lot of letters from a wide range of people. You can have no idea what a joy it is, as an inmate, to receive a letter from an old friend out of the blue, telling you about their kids, what's going on in their life, and including you in it and hoping that you are fit and well. Many people wrote once or twice, and that was more than sufficient, believe me – just to know that you hadn't been forgotten was enough. To all those who did head for the hills, I always remember the line from George Orwell's famous novel *Animal Farm*: "And the pig got up and slowly walked away"!

One inmate who stood out because he was so inconspicuous was Christopher Hall. I know that might sound odd but the mere fact of his introversion made him noticeable. Christopher Hall is a serial rapist and was serving a huge sentence. Hall did nothing with his time except watch television, was not involved in any activities and was merely marking time until his release. My belief is that people like this should not be released unless they have undergone compulsory sex offenders' programs – and even these can be useless in some cases. I really wonder whether chemical or physical castration for these violent recidivist sex offenders is not an answer.

In any event Hall was a mate of Camilleri's, and together they formed the core of the crew opposing Dupas et al. For some reason Camilleri had a real set against Dupas and it was mutual. There was a constant power struggle between them. They would not talk, they would not eat near each other. They would not even stand in the medication line together. This created huge pressure in the unit, and on more than one occasion there were fights. As I've said, Camilleri is a big man but can't fight. Dupas is a small man, fat, but with immense power in his hands. He is a very dangerous person. He would not fight toe to toe; he would wait his chance and jump you. That is the sort of person he is.

Dean Rayment, also one of the Dupas crew, had murdered Cindy Ward many, many years ago and when I met him he had served fifteen years. He is now released back into the community. One wonders why. "Dino" was illiterate to the degree that he could not fill out his canteen form each week without the help of Peter Dupas. Dupas even used to roll his smokes for him and all the time Dino had spent in jail, he had not been required to do any education. He was not a sex offender so didn't have to do that program, and surprisingly began his supervised day leaves before his release from maximum security at Port Phillip. The leave program is designed to help prisoners who have served more than three years minimum to re-integrate into society. I was in jail with Dino when he was taken on his first leave after thirteen-odd years in custody. He is a chronic epileptic and is on heavy, heavy medication. He would do nothing the entire day except sit either outside smoking or in his cell watching television. He was medicated to the eyeballs and went home, I understand, to live with his aged grandmother.

Dino's leave was, believe it or not, into the central business district of the city of Melbourne, where he went to McDonald's for the first time and then to the pictures. Can anybody explain to me how sitting in a darkened picture theatre for a couple of hours helps you re-integrate into society? This whole exercise backfired as poor Dino, being "out" for the first time in thirteen years, could not cope with the crowds or the pace of the place and freaked out in McDonald's, dropped his burger and bolted upstairs to a quieter area. How do I know this? The screw who took Dino on the leave told me the same day.

To say Dino was a mess would be an understatement. As I've already said he is a chronic epileptic, and one day they took him off his epilepsy medication. The almost immediate result was that Dino, at the top of the stairs on the first tier of the unit, had a fit and fell down these steel stairs to the bottom. Nobody knew what to do, including the screws. I rolled him onto his side, and we just had to let the fit run its course. He got up and was taken to the doctor – and was placed back on his medication.

Another one of the Dupas crew was Mark England, known as Biff. Biff was doing twenty-three years for the murder and necrophilia of a grandmother in Geelong. He burgled her house searching for money to buy drugs, murdered the grandmother, then after she was dead had sex with her. He found some money and spent it on drugs, went back and repeated the process again, except on this occasion he tried to burn the house down for good measure. This poor woman had been left dead in her house for a couple of days.

To show you how smart Biff was, he appealed against his

conviction and his sentence and opened his appeal by berating the court, whereupon the judge promptly gave him an extra two years for contempt. If there is ever a move that is not very smart it is to abuse the court when you are seeking that very same court's leniency.

Biff too was virtually illiterate, and was only in his early twenties when convicted. He had a very long sentence to go, and on rare occasions would come and work with Dupas and me in the garden. He would swing the mattock for a few minutes, break into a sweat and then head back inside, and continue to do nothing, as was his wont.

Biff is a classic example of what is wrong with jail. As a young man with a long sentence, rather than give him nothing to do, he should be subject to compulsory education, compulsory life skills and compulsory counselling. In addition he was morbidly obese. There is no compulsory physical fitness regime for such prisoners, and no proper diet, so he was allowed to just blow out. I was with Biff for fifteen months and not once did I see him with an educator or a counsellor. This leaves society in exactly the same position upon his release as it was when he went in. That is, exposed to somebody who is a murderer and a necrophile who is more than likely, due to their inability to cope, to murder again. If he's educated and properly counselled and effectively re-programmed, it may well be different, but until these things are attended to, these sorts of things will continue to happen and society is the ultimate loser.

One of the blokes I had real difficulty coming to terms with seeing in jail was Christopher Empey. He had previously been the state manager for Elders in Tasmania. He was married and had a young child who was born while he was in custody. Out of the blue, in a drunken rage while at a conference at Crown Casino, he violently attacked a female colleague, raped her and bashed her to such a degree that she was lucky to survive. Other injuries were inflicted on her which are frankly too terrible to recount here.

When I met Empey I couldn't work out why somebody who seemed so normal would behave in such a way. It appears, however, that over the years he had had trouble with binge drinking, would suffer blackouts and all these blackout episodes culminated in these offences taking place. He will have a very long time to come to terms with what he did. His life is ruined. He was gradually taken into the Dupas crew as well.

The two odd bods in the unit were Carlos Cabal and his brother-in-law Marco Pasini. These two blokes were Mexican bankers who had fled Mexico after allegedly having ripped off billions of dollars from the Mexican Government. What followed was a legal circus of monumental proportions. Both Cabal and Pasini moved to Melbourne, where they bought houses and were living a normal life (if you call living the life of Riley normal) until the shit hit the fan and they were arrested on extradition warrants from Mexico. The pair of them were placed in Sirius East for their own protection because of the money they supposedly had.

Well, what a great place to put somebody who needs protection; you are placing them in custody with blokes who have absolutely nothing to lose and everything to gain by having a billionaire in the next cell. Raymond Edmunds quite happily told me that he had extracted $200,000 from Cabal to "look after him" while he was in custody. Another prisoner received $10,000 to swap cells, and on it goes. Both of these admissions were made directly to me by the prisoners concerned, who proudly boasted how much they had been able to extract from the two "suckers", as they described them.

Cabal, who fought his extradition, had a team of lawyers that you couldn't jump over, and ultimately returned to Mexico after a couple of years to be acquitted of all charges. He ended up doing a couple of years for nothing. When I arrived at Port Phillip, Pasini was still there. He was a very quiet bloke and kept to himself. Nobody went near him because money is power. He was able to look after himself by way of the protection he was able to purchase.

It was always interesting to me that I could not even get bananas in jail, although I offered to pay for them. What transpired was a farce. The authorities repeatedly refused to provide me with bananas, until I threatened to take them to court on the basis that I was being discriminated against. The Jewish, the Muslim and the vegetarian prisoners were all given bananas but I as a WASP was refused them. So therefore I was being discriminated against. Mention the magic word *discrimination* and all of a sudden everything becomes possible. Within a couple of hours I had my bananas, and I continued to receive them weekly after that. I hasten to add that I was being charged approximately five times the going rate for those bananas each week. What is the point of complaining? You just kick along with it.

In view of the great banana debacle I was always interested to see the fine array of Mexican food available inside supposedly the most secure unit, inside the most secure jail. How did it get there? Only one possible explanation: prison officers.

Interestingly one of the prison officers got to go to Mexico at that time. Lucky I guess. The two Mexicans kept very much to themselves, and were not aligned with any of the factions within the unit. They didn't need to be; they had money.

There were other blokes in the unit. like Mick Hall, who was an armed robber and a hard man. He was there because he couldn't help himself: every time he was arrested he would, for some reason, become a compulsive talker, and drop everybody else in the poo along with him. This made him very unpopular, to say the least, with other prisoners, and accordingly he could not go into mainstream, for fear of the physical ill that would be befall him from other prisoners he had informed on. This made for difficult times in the unit, because he considered himself to be above all of these other scumbags, who were mainly in for sex offences. Mick was what in jail jargon is known as a "Ten slap job": one slap to start him talking, then nine to stop him!

Another bloke called Mick (not Mick Hall) was in for a murder committed over a drug deal gone wrong when the delivery driver had been chained to a tree and shot more than once. There were a number of accused and Mick had dropped all of them in the shit along with himself. As the trial approached you could see the pressure mount. Where was the hard bastard who strutted about the unit telling everyone he was a bikie? One night just before the trial there was one hell of a to-do in the unit very late. All I could hear was someone saying "stay with me Mick" over and over. It turns out the brave man had slashed his arms from elbow to wrist and had nearly bled out when he called for help. As it turns out it was lucky he did set off the emergency alarm and it worked (surprisingly), because all were acquitted at the conclusion of the trial! You can always tell when someone is fair dinkum about suicide because they don't cut across their wrists, they cut down. It is harder to stop the bleeding and to repair the veins.

There was also another category of crook in Sirius East at the time: those who didn't need protection from the rest of the prison; rather, the rest of the prison system needed protection from them. They were blokes who had such short fuses that they were likely to go off and belt anybody at any time. I had the privilege of sharing the space with a couple of such blokes. One was a particularly violent bloke called Austin Kildea. Austin was, to be polite, not playing with a full deck and used to let his fists do the talking rather than try to intellectualise his way out of anything. As a result, poor old Aussie was kept in protection for many years, and if the medication was late or didn't arrive, as was so often the case, he would go off, more often than not belting into a screw.

One day, when I was in another part of the jail, I saw Aussie being dragged off to the slot (solitary confinement) after belting yet another screw. Six officers were carrying him horizontal to the footpath, face-down. His hands were cuffed behind him and his legs were cuffed together. As the officers walked along, the ones in front dropped his face onto the ground and the others behind just kept pushing. You can imagine what that did to Austin's face. Not good. Of course, prisoners who had a tendency to belt the screws were given a very wide berth, and the screws only went near them when absolutely necessary, for obvious reasons.

There were a couple of other prisoners in this category, one of whom I used to play footy with. When, to quote him, he "chinned" one of the supervisors one evening, I was singled out for special treatment on the basis that I knew him. That's the sort of logic that applies in jail.

There were other blokes in the unit of a similar ilk, whose names I can't remember. To give you an idea of the terrific blokes we had in there, there was a very old man who was in for raping his adult son. There was another bloke who was in for raping his daughter and he was so competent that he had shot himself in the head nine times with a nail gun, yes nine times, and hadn't killed himself! How on earth can you do that to yourself and not take your own life? You can imagine what sort of a state this bloke was in. He was not travelling at all well and wouldn't have anything to do with anybody else. He was a cave dweller – in other words, he came out of his cell for food or medication; the rest of the time he sat in his darkened cell with the curtains drawn.

There was just one other category of inmate: those prisoners who were suffering obvious mental conditions and should patently not be in jail. A classic example was a bloke called Joe Smith. I'm telling you about Joe out of pity for Joe and my complete disgust with the system. I liked Joe and felt sorry for him. He had an unfortunate family background and was a chronic schizophrenic. All he did was take his medication and train on the weights. Joe was a huge man with massive strength. That strength was so breathtaking that, when Joe had a bad day mentally, everybody headed for the hills. Why was he in jail, you may ask. Well, ask any Australian State government why people like Joe are in jail rather than in mental institutions and you won't get an answer. It was Mr Kennett who gutted the mental health system in Victoria and put the Joe Smiths of this world out on the street where it's an iron clad certainty that they'll commit offences and end up in the nick. Precisely the place they shouldn't be.

On one of Joe's bad days, he started complaining that everybody was staring at him and talking about him on muster. That was always a sign that he was about to go "off". Muster was concluded, nothing done … no one talks to Joe to try and calm him down; all the screws are terrified of him, so they leave him alone. The next thing the telly comes flying out of Joe's cell door, which was on the first tier, and smashes on the floor in the middle of the unit. Joe follows, catapulting out of his cell, and starts barking at everybody, completely unintelligibly. Next Joey jumps from the top tier down onto the billiard table, then onto the floor like some sort of demented ape, screaming and shouting, his eyes out on stalks. He then races up to his cell. The screws follow him and lock the door. What happens next?

Easy, the screws come and get the prison listener. A prison listener is another prisoner who has some training in counselling and who then talks to prisoners about any particular problems that they might not want to talk to doctors, psychologists or prison officers about. I was a prison listener in that unit and the screws came to my cell and asked me whether I would go and talk to Joey. Needless to say I was apprehensive.

I went up to Joe's cell. The screws opened the cell door, and there was Joe sitting in the corner like a caged animal. I must say that, looking back now, I don't think I would do this again. As I have said, Joe was immensely strong, and he could have snapped me in half if he felt like it. Instead he was sitting there like a kid. I walked in, and said to him, "Joey, it's Andrew, I'm your friend, you know. Let's have a chat about whatever the problem is." Joe looked at me and my heart was in my mouth. Luckily everything went the right way and Joe calmed down sufficiently for the nurses to get some medication into him, which effectively knocked him rotten. He was then taken to the hospital.

Joey was eventually released, and I've since found out that he was uncomfortable back in society. He committed more offences, and is now back in jail where he is more comfortable. This is a crying shame. This bloke needs help. He needs to be looked after. He doesn't need to be locked in a maximum security prison every time he offends. He never gets leaves, which are designed to help people re-integrate. Why? Because everyone's too terrified to take him on leaves; so he gets no counselling, nothing to help him re-integrate into society. He merely concludes his sentence, then the door is opened and out he walks, back into the world that he is not ready for. What happens? He can't cope. He reoffends. Put back into jail, released again and so the merry-go-round continues forever for poor Joe Smith. Joey, if you read this book, I'm saying these things about you in a compassionate manner because I really like you. Joe Smith looked out for me while I was in jail, but he should be in an institution where he can be looked after properly.

Joe Smith wasn't the only prisoner who fell into that category. That's why this has become a pet issue of mine: I saw far too many mentally ill people in jail. It is a disgrace. Nobody says anything about it. And when I start up, everybody hopes I will go away. I won't. I will continue agitating until somebody does something for these people.

The other important aspect of life in Sirius East was, of course, the screws. These officers tended to be the more experienced officers, placed into a unit which was highly volatile. There were a lot of old Pentridge screws there. Pentridge Prison was the now defunct maximum security prison in Coburg in Melbourne. It was a Dickensian prison, all bluestone, buggery and violence, and these officers had spent their working lives in that hardened environment. Not quite the appropriate qualification to bring new hope to prisoners in the modern-day prison. Old-fashioned screws set in their old-fashioned Dickensian violent and lazy ways … what hope rehabilitation?

I look around the unit and wonder how the lunatics have been left in charge of the asylum. This is surely going to be an interesting time for young Andrew!

Chapter 3

Lunatic Soup, "Sausagegate" and Random Observations

Grandpa pissed his pants again
He don't give a damn
Brother Billy has both guns drawn.
He ain't been right since Vietnam.

– WARREN ZEVON, *PLAY IT ALL NIGHT LONG*

Toby Fraser (no relation) was considered by everybody in Sirius East to be nothing but a pest. Toby was about twenty when I met him and had been in and out of jail for drug- and alcohol-related offences for most of his adult life. He had been in boys' homes before that. He was in jail because he had robbed a couple of teenagers on the beach at Frankston while in an alcohol- and drug-induced state. After the robbery he had poured some lighter fluid on one of the victims and stood there with a cigarette lighter threatening to ignite him. For that Toby received a sentence of imprisonment, which was subject to appeal at the time I met him.

To date, Toby had received extraordinarily light sentences because – as is the way of the Children's Court – he had been treated extremely leniently. He had serious problems in an adult jail, mainly because of his general demeanour. His trick, because he had no money, was to borrow from other prisoners with the promise that he would repay them on canteen day, which was once a week. Of course, when canteen day came, there was no repayment. Toby would then proceed to borrow from somebody else in the unit to square off with the previous week's benefactor. Don't forget that when the music stops there is always someone left without a chair, so the rort always came to an end when Toby ran out of creditors. The debt was always for White Ox roll-your-own tobacco, which is about as rough as Hessian underpants, and that is only to smell! Tobacco is real currency within the jail, even if you don't smoke. Most things can be purchased for a small or large pouch of "Ox". Once Toby had exhausted all means of rorting in that unit, he would "bail" to another unit. This meant he would say he was in danger in that particular unit and then be moved to another unit within the protection area. He would wait for the prisoners that he had short-changed to be sent to other units or jails, then he would go back to that unit and start his little scam all over again. Due to his notorious behaviour he had no friends and was constantly getting a smack in the mouth from older prisoners. As one bloke said to me, "It's only a rort if you're not in it!"

Toby befriended me because he probably saw me as an easy touch. However, I was never sucked in to his little schemes and accordingly he would sit for some time talking to me about his problems and how he would be going home immediately after his appeal. He repeatedly stated he wouldn't be drinking any more and that he was a reformed person. When you have these discussions in jail, which you do frequently, you always take them with a grain of salt. Most of it is crap and the blokes have absolutely no intention of reforming, let alone never offending again. As proof of this Toby was the designated unit brewer of "lunatic soup". Lunatic soup is the home brew that is cooked up by prisoners within the jail. This was one way he could ingratiate himself with the other prisoners.

Bearing in mind that we were in maximum security, protection from protection, it never ceased to amaze me how slack the prison officers were and how easy it was for Toby to brew up a batch of lunatic soup.

The only equipment required was a large plastic empty tomato sauce bottle with half gallon capacity. The crucial ingredient was bread, which has some live yeast remaining in it even after cooking and is enough to get a fermentation happening. The brewer would soak the bread until fermentation began, then cram it into the neck of the bottle together with whatever sliced fruit was available – usually oranges and orange peel – add sugar and water, and put the lid on. The favourite place to hide the bottle while the brew was taking place was in one of the large plastic rubbish bins in the unit. Twice a day, the bin billet responsible takes the liner full of rubbish out of the bin and replaces it with a fresh liner. The first time I was the bin billet I noticed the tomato sauce bottle and was told in no uncertain terms that it was not to be touched. The procedure was merely to put a fresh liner in the bin over the bottle and leave it alone. This I did. I don't know how long the brew took, but it certainly wasn't long, because a little while later there was quite some excitement in the unit as the word got around that the brew was ready.

I was sitting in my cell when Toby lurched in holding his china cup and asked me if I wanted a drink. The smell was putrid. It was like that of a fermenting compost heap and when I looked in the cup I saw a milky-grey liquid. Toby was clearly drunk, as was just about everybody else in the unit. He strongly recommended the drink, adding "Have a look how much alcohol's in it!" With that, he pulled out his cigarette lighter and held it near the top of the cup. Immediately a blue flame burst forth from the cup. I couldn't believe my eyes. These blokes were drinking a very, very powerful brew, strong enough to keep most of the unit pissed for a couple of days. And to think: the screws were watching the whole time as somebody walked around with a large tomato sauce bottle full of liquid. How that happened and nobody asked what was in it, I do not know. I don't mind enjoying the odd glass of red, as I am now while I write this book, but this stuff was beyond the pale ... and I didn't need the dose of the trots that always followed a good dose of lunatic soup! So I never touched the stuff.

The lunatic soup was a big hit – and boy, did it ever turn the partakers into lunatics. There were blokes falling over, blokes asleep and blokes hardly able to stand up on muster. All this happening in a maximum security prison!

Toby was sharing a cell with another youngster called Chris Reynolds. Chris's claim to fame was that he, like Toby, clearly liked playing with fire as he had fatally incinerated a homeless person on the banks of the Murray River at Mildura.

Chris had never been in jail before and was not coping at all well – that's why he was placed in a protected unit, and placed in with Toby. They were left well alone so that they could do the brew, because everybody wanted a drink.

Anyone who was young was constantly being harassed by older prisoners for sex. Unfortunately one young bloke was out in the yard with the rest of us one day, assembling Dynabolts, when he was grabbed by an older prisoner who was in jail for rape. He was dragged into the toilet in the workroom where he was bashed and his anus slit open with a razor blade, then he was raped in full view of everybody else.

How does this happen in a maximum security prison? Well, let me explain the layout of Sirius East (with apologies to those who have read about this in my previous book). As you walk into the unit the first thing you see is the officers' station, then there is the unit itself, which would be, at a guess, 20 metres long. You then walk out to an exercise yard known as the "chook pen", which is approximately 6 to 12 metres wide. After you cross the chook pen there is a prefabricated concrete workroom with a toilet off it which had no windows in it, and just one door. While the prisoners were assembling the nuts and bolts no officers were on duty in that room, ever. The officers, at best, were about 30 metres away and a designated prisoner always sat at the work table looking back into the unit and towards the officers' station. The minute an officer looked like moving in the general direction of the workroom, the word would be given and whatever nefarious activity was taking place would cease.

Sexual assault wasn't the only thing that took place in the workroom. Other prisoners were bashed there, particularly Andrew Davies. As I said earlier everybody seemed to think that it was alright to be in jail for murdering a defenceless woman, as Dupas and Camilleri had, yet to be a paedophile like Davies was reprehensible. The workroom was also where the "shivs" (jail knives) were made. There were some old wheelchairs stored in that room, for some reason, and every possible brace or piece of steel that could be removed was removed and was then filed on the floor of the workroom to a sharp point, to be used on other prisoners at some stage in the future.

Following the rape the young man completely lost his mind and was placed in the acute unit, where I visited him on a number of occasions. He was kept drugged to the eyeballs by the powers that be there – so much so that, on a couple of occasions when I went in to visit, he was unable to get off his bed. His eyes were glazed and he was starring at the ceiling. It is interesting that these categories of offences never seem to be publicised by the prison system. I was told that he had been offered a substantial amount of money by the jail as compensation for the attack, but on the basis that there was a non-disclosure clause in the settlement, so he had to keep his mouth shut. He later settled with the jail but that has never been made public. Whatever happened to accountability?

The one question I have been constantly asked since leaving jail is about jail sex. Every bloke seems to have a morbid fascination with the subject. I am regularly asked whether I was raped or sexually assaulted. I am pleased to report that I wasn't. The closest I came to an incident was after I had been moved to Fulham, near Sale. I had finished my daily run and because it was a nice day I was doing my stretching on the lawn outside my cottage. A bloke who was in for murdering his boyfriend when he discovered him in bed with another bloke had taken a bit of a shine to me, even though I was old enough to be his father. Jamie walked past me as I was stretching and said, "Oh, I could just about squeeze in there." To which I replied: "Jamie, you couldn't get a grain of rice up my arse!" Jamie: "It's not the rice you have to worry about, it's what I am going to push it in with!" Needless to say I beat a dignified retreat to my room, where I locked the door until my fancier had gone away and cooled down.

A further example of the violence in jail, and the constant covering up of it, was the case of a young chap in a medical unit at Port Phillip. He was sitting reading the newspaper in the pool room when a fight broke out at the billiard table behind him and he was attacked from behind with a billiard cue. He was severely injured and to this day has a number of steel plates inserted in his skull. That particular prisoner is now in a protection prison, on the basis that if he were attacked again and received a blow to the scone, it would probably kill him. So he has been placed, unfortunately for him, with an old paedophile who at least is non-violent. When this young man made a claim against Port Phillip Prison, it was fought on the basis that he had contributed, in some way that was never explained, to his own assault. As a former lawyer, I fail to see how somebody sitting with their back to a fight, reading the newspaper, has contributed to a severe assault occasioned on them without warning.

The jail has now settled with that young man and paid him a substantial amount of money for the injuries he sustained, but again subject to the signing of a non-disclosure agreement. Whatever happens, we cannot possibly allow the general public to know how the prisons that are paid for with taxpayers' money are operated. In such cases, non-

42

disclosure agreements are not because the matters are commercial-in-confidence; they are a cover-up, plain and simple, and should not be allowed. (This concept should also apply to all government contracts and agreements. In my view it is outrageous that contracts are entered into by governments – who, after all, are technically employed by us the taxpayers – without the entire contract process being open to scrutiny. The cynic in me always smells a rat when a politician claims commercial-in-confidence in refusing to disclose details of contracts entered into on our behalf. What have they got to hide?)

Don't forget the other matters that are hushed up as well and which appear all the worse for the cover-up once they are inevitably exposed. One example is the asthmatic who died after pushing the panic button at Port Phillip Prison – and, as per usual, the panic button didn't work. The asthmatic's name was Ian Thomas Campbell Westcott. Westcott was a 55-year-old white-collar criminal who was on remand (that is, he was refused bail before his trial) and had not yet even been convicted, so the presumption of innocence was still in his favour. Westcott had an asthma attack after lockdown one night and was suffering for so long that he was able to write and leave a note to the effect that he had died as a result of not being able to get any help in the middle of the night because nobody answered his call. The note was reported as saying: "asthma attack, buzzed for help, no response". This ended up before the Coroner, and

Port Phillip Prison was accused of a gross dereliction of responsibility.

What an outrage! Here is a bloke, who (by the way) has not even been convicted, dying because of another stuff-up. (Not that a conviction would make any life less valuable.) Why no buzzer? Negligence? Refusal to pay for repairs? Or not caring? Take your pick – it has to be one or all three of these. I suspect all three. This episode also explains why Camilleri was never charged after he attacked another prisoner with a pitchfork. Not caught on camera, as I had been told by one of the screws – probably because the camera wasn't working. Where is the accountability?

Toby Fraser's appeal was refused and he was ordered to serve his total sentence. Significantly, all the time I was with Toby I did not see him receive a skerrick of counselling, a scrap of education, or anything at all that could be remotely construed as beneficial to him or society.

Toby was subsequently released and I heard nothing further from him until I myself was released early in return for agreeing to become a Crown witness against Peter Dupas. Toby somehow found my mother's telephone number, rang her and threatened her that he was going to come around and bash her because I was giving evidence against his mate, Peter Dupas. My mother is the quintessential middle-class mum who has never been exposed to people like Toby. You can imagine the impact this effort had on a woman of mum's age and background! Profound, to say the least.

The Homicide Squad were advised and immediately became involved but Toby couldn't be found. Bearing in mind his previous behaviour, it seemed that these threats were all hot air as Toby had no ticker and would never act on the threats – or at least that's what we thought at the time.

I subsequently gave evidence against Dupas and never heard a word of Toby Fraser again until December 2007 when I picked up the newspaper and nearly fell off the chair. A man called Toby Fraser – from the photo, clearly one and the same Toby that I was in with – had been jailed in the Supreme Court of Western Australia for bludgeoning a 44-year-old man on the beach near Exmouth in northern Western Australia in October 2006. According to this chronology, not long after I was released and not long after Toby had made the phone call to my mother, he was murdering somebody in cold blood. The chilling aspect of this murder was that, after Toby had bludgeoned the victim, he strangled him with a piece of rope while he was still semi-conscious and sang to his victim a song by a band called Slayer which used the line "Look into my eyes while you die."

Toby was later found to own a DVD of the violent Hollywood film *Natural Born Killers*. As in that movie, there was no rational reason for murder, and there was no clear motive for Toby to have murdered this man, who had in fact befriended him by picking him up as a hitchhiker.

Toby had already been on a crime spree in Western Australia after leaving Victoria. After the beach murder,

Toby and his girlfriend stole the deceased's credit card and seven cans of beer from his car and chucked his body into the sea. The two later bought chicken parmigiana and a bottle of bourbon for dinner, then paid for a motel room, all with the deceased's credit card. Not the smartest thing to do if you want to avoid apprehension. Toby said when the police arrested him that he had been drinking heavily before the murder and had also been using testosterone, a steroid and a male growth hormone. This is rather interesting because Toby was tall and very weedy, and, as I said, had been stood over regularly. My bet is that he was taking the testosterone in a vain attempt to try and bulk up to avoid any further problems.

Toby was sentenced to twenty-seven years in prison and his girlfriend received four years and eight months for being an accessory to the murder. The thing that staggers me is the rapid progression of somebody like Toby from being just a dishonest, conniving pest, as I described him at the start of this chapter, to being a cold, callous, calculating killer. Knowing Toby Fraser as I do, I am unable to comprehend how he could stare into the eyes of a fellow human being while quietly strangling them, singing them a song and, with the other hand, pretending he was calling an ambulance. It is probably better that somebody like Toby will not see the light of day again, because if he continues as he had in prison when I was with him, he will not see out his sentence – he will be killed in jail.

There was one episode in jail that has never ceased to amuse me. It was the talk of the entire prison system once the cat was out of the bag.

There is a unit at Port Phillip which is also a quasi protection unit called Marlborough, which is for the mentally infirm. Once again I emphasise that Marlborough inmates are precisely the people who should not be in jail; rather, they should be in secure mental health facilities. Of course, nobody will bother to address this issue.

It is generally accepted that all the blokes in Marlborough have a few roos loose in the top paddock and therefore would not be able to cope in the general prison population. The most popular Marlborough prisoner was an African who was in jail for having sex with domestic cats – yes, cats! He was silly enough to tell someone else this story and of course the story raced around the jail like a bushfire! Every time he would be escorted around the jail or have a visit with his parents there would be cat calls (forgive the pun) of "Here puss, puss" or blokes making meowing noises. While I felt sorry for the bloke, it was very funny in an environment where there was not a lot of levity.

One poor Marlborough prisoner was the subject of a supposed prank by four prison officers. The so-called prank came about when the officers concerned told the prisoner that it was his turn to leave the jail with the screws to get the doughnuts for the unit that week. To show you how gullible this young man was, no doughnuts are brought in from the outside, ever, for any prisoner. That clearly didn't cross his mind, and he didn't have the mental capacity to intellectualise the fact that there were no doughnuts, ever. He fell for it and was very excited at the prospect of going outside the prison to buy a treat for the unit.

The officers told the prisoner that, before he could go out, however, he had to participate in a security drill, which involved him inserting up his bum a sausage from the kitchen wrapped in a bit of glad wrap. He would then see if he could get through the security at the front door to go outside the jail and purchase the doughnuts without the staff at the front gate discovering the "contraband". What followed was that the prisoner stuck the sausage into his anus and went with the officers to the front gate, where he was immediately strip searched. As happens in a strip search, once you are naked you are ordered to turn around and bend over and part your cheeks (about as demeaning as it gets) – "smile for the Governor", as it's called – and lo and behold there was the end of the sausage sticking out of this kid's bottom.

Apparently this preying on a gullible young person by precisely those employed to protect him was a source of great hilarity. A photograph was taken of the sausage in situ and the young man was allegedly threatened with being charged with trying to remove an item from the jail. Needless to say, as he had failed the bogus security drill, there were no doughnuts for little Johnny and he was sent back to his unit.

LUNATIC SOUP, "SAUSAGEGATE" AND RANDOM OBSERVATIONS

All the screws thought this was a huge joke and this story got around the jail very quickly.

This would not have gone any further had the young fellow not casually mentioned to his parents on his next visit that he had failed a security drill during the week and hadn't got any doughnuts. Once the parents heard this all hell broke loose and the senior supervising officer involved, Mr (he always insisted on being addressed as "Mr") Trevor Spearman, endeavoured to cover up the whole incident on behalf of the other three officers. (By the way, I was always taught that respect is something that is earned, not demanded. So much for MR Spearman!) All four officers concerned were stood down and there was an investigation.

The wash-up of this so-called "Sausagegate" was that the young man has now, I understand, received a substantial payout by the prison and the officers were all sacked. Can anybody therefore explain to me how, when I was at Melbourne Airport recently, I spotted Trevor Spearman checking hand luggage and clothing at the departure gate? Believe it or not, Mr Spearman is still working in the security industry, actually X-raying your luggage, coats, shoes, etc. before you board a plane to depart Melbourne. How does Trevor (Mr no more!) have a job in the security industry after being dismissed for being prepared to cover up the incident? I suppose it's because there are very few sausages exported from the passenger terminal at Melbourne Airport!

What amazes me more is the fact that this young man was taken from his unit without any proper paperwork. He was taken to the front door of the jail without any paperwork at all, and was then submitted to this unnecessary humiliation by officers, all supposedly in the name of a bit of fun. The preying on the weak by an officer who is trained to know better is inexcusable.

I noted with interest that one of the other officers dismissed over "Sausagegate" was an officer by the name of Russell Davies. Mr Davies had an unpleasant disposition and clearly didn't like his job at all. One evening I had finished a visit with my family, and I was coming back out to the strip room where you are taken out of the monkey suit that you wear on a visit and then strip searched. The monkey suit is a one-piece garment with a zip up the back with a cable tie placed around the top of the zip, the theory being to stop you secreting any contraband around your person. It clearly doesn't work because the entire jail is riddled with drugs. However, the procedure is that you come out from your visit, you take your key off the key ring board, unlock your locker and take your clothes into the strip room where you are strip searched. After the strip search you head back to your unit.

I followed this usual procedure and Mr Davies, without warning, started screaming abuse, venting a tirade of fuck this and fuck that upon me. It was all to do with me taking the key off the key rack. I was absolutely dumbfounded at his attitude, and I told him in no uncertain terms. A hush descended over the entire strip room because not many prisoners spoke back to the officers. There were three other officers on duty there and they all said nothing. The crooks thought there might be some fun and games as a consequence, so they all stuck their heads around the corner into the strip room to see what was going on.

Davies screamed at me that the procedure wasn't to (fucking this and fucking that) take the keys off the key rack, but rather for the officer to do it. Talk about a storm in a tea cup. I had been in jail about two years by this time and that was the first occasion on which this alleged procedure had ever been outlined to me. I was merely following the practice that I'd been following whenever I had received a visit. Nevertheless, Davies continued to scream abuse and berate me, becoming so red in the face that I thought he was going to blow a valve. I just stood there.

I made every attempt I could not to infuriate the screws for obvious reasons, and this bloke's berating out of the blue really shocked me.

We subsequently went into the strip room and he conducted the strip search. As I was leaving I said to him: "I want you to remember one thing. One day my sentence will be over. I will go home and I will work hard to make a success of myself once again. In the meantime you will still be here looking up blokes' arses in the strip room!" I did not know at that time how prescient my comments were but after Sausagegate it became clear that Mr Davies had gone one step further than just *looking* up blokes' arses!

The next day I was on my run when Davies appeared in the compound where I was running and walked over. He said he wanted to talk to me about what had happened last night. I said to him "Is this official business?" He said "No." I said, "Don't talk to me ever again unless it's on official business" and I kept running. I looked back as I was running around and he was still standing there clearly nonplussed by my reply.

If you stick to your guns and let them know that you are not prepared to be walked over, or stood over, then by and large the officers are essentially gutless bullies and only prey on the weak.

While on the subject of officers, the other aspect that is perennially kept quiet is the issue of trafficking of contraband by officers to prisoners. It is not just drugs, it is general contraband. Pornography can be purchased, even alcohol can be purchased. While I was at Fulham, a medium and minimum security prison, you were at some stages able to buy for $100 a bottle of Johnny Walker Red Label Scotch whisky, which at that time had a retail of less than $20. Some blokes were that desperate for a drink that they paid their $100, particularly around New Year's eve.

The big ticket item, of course, is drugs. Drugs are trafficked within the jail not only by crooks but by officers. Yet again it surprises me the lengths that the authorities go

LUNATIC SOUP, "SAUSAGEGATE" AND RANDOM OBSERVATIONS

to, and by this I mean the Office of Corrections generally, to hush up these misdemeanours. The obvious reason for the hush-up is that it reflects badly on the system, as it should.

In my previous book I talked about fellow inmates trying to sell me drugs, and prison officers attempted to as well. In Port Phillip it is on for young and old, it's every man for himself in the drug trafficking department! As it turns out, both the prison officers who tried to sell me drugs have been charged with trafficking and have been dismissed from the prison service. How long had the trafficking been going on? The answer is: quite some time. It was common knowledge that these officers were selling drugs, and if that was the case, and all the prisoners knew, how come it took the authorities so long to wake up to it?

The first time I was offered drugs by an officer was when I was walking back from the gymnasium one day while I was in Sirius East. Because I was in maximum protection I could not go anywhere through the main part of the jail without being escorted by an officer. There were just the two of us and we were chatting away about football and he said to me, "Are you right for everything? "Yeah, I'm pretty right." He said, "Well, are you right for *everything?*" with the emphasis on "everything". I looked at him and said, "What do you mean?" He said, "Do you need any drugs?" He was as blatant as that and I thought it was a setup. In any event I was well and truly clean of drugs by then and, as now, and I wanted nothing to do with them. Even so, he said if I changed my mind he could easily get me some cocaine. He told me it would be $4,000 for half an ounce or $600 for a gram. He was quite specific about the type of drug and the amounts and the cost. I declined his kind offer and nothing further was said about.

Another prison officer at Port Phillip was charged too. She and I had had a similar conversation one day when I was being escorted to the gym. I was not the only prisoner this happened to; it happened regularly.

While on the subject of the gym and prison officers, what about the prisoner who was having sex with a female gym guard? The shit hit the fan well and truly, the crook being shipped off to the slot and the screw getting the heave-ho. This was not an isolated incident. Another bloke, Joe, with whom I had been in Sirius East was moved out of protection to a medium security prison and, hey presto, started horizontal folk dancing with one of the female staff, the inevitable result being that young Joe was sent back to Port Phillip for a cold shower or two!

One officer at Fulham suicided in the prison car park after he had been found in possession of child pornography.

It was blindingly obvious that the gymnasium was the handover point. I have seen packages change hands there that were obviously drugs because of the size of the package and the way in which it was slipped from one hand to the next. Easy to miss, but equally easy to spot if you know what you are looking for. With my history of drug abuse and the clandestine nature of the drug industry, it was apparent to me what was happening. Once a crook had scored he would head for the toilet and "boot" the drugs (stick them up his bum) and then head back to the unit where it was party time!

It's interesting that, since I raised the issue, in my last book, of officers selling drugs and of drugs in jail, not one person has come out and said that I am lying. I find that an extraordinary acceptance of guilt by omission. Have these officers been dealt with by the courts, and what penalty was imposed, if any? Have you seen a result published in the media? I haven't.

The other random observation I wish to make doesn't surround the prison officers and the way the prison is run, but rather the genesis of some of the prisoners and some of the trends that appeared to emerge. The one that interested me the most was the number of ex-servicemen in custody for crimes of violence. In particular, there were four blokes in there who were all ex-army. All in for shooting murders. Three were in for indiscriminate murders and the fourth was in there for a totally irrational piece of behaviour which resulted in a murder and one attempted murder.

One of them, Julian Knight, is infamous in the state of Victoria as the Hoddle Street killer. He murdered a number of people in cold blood, for no apparent reason, in Hoddle Street one night many years ago. Knight is in custody and there he shall remain until he shuffles off this mortal coil.

On its own this is not so interesting, but the second army person I came into contact with in Sirius East was Andrew Norrie, another member of the Dupas crew. Norrie was a former soldier who had been hitchhiking to Victoria from Queensland when he was picked up by a couple. Norrie murdered these charitable people, who had picked him up out of the goodness of their hearts. One of the victims had been made to run through the bush while Norrie and his co-accused had pot shots at them, just like at target practice.

The third was Bobby "the Batsman" Pickford, so called for his serial self abuse that went on day and night. I know because I was in the next room and could hear! Bob had also been hitchhiking after discharge from the army and had murdered a mum and dad, yet again for no apparent reason, had sex with both people after they were dead, and kept their bodies in the back of their utility, which he stole and drove away from the scene of the crimes. Some weeks later the Batsman was brought undone by a Vietnam veteran who, when walking down Darlinghurst Road in Sydney, smelt a stench coming from the car. Being a Vietnam veteran he knew precisely what that stench was and called the police. Pickford has now done twenty-three or twenty-four years and I understand he is just about to be released or has been released.

I happened to live with Pickford at Fulham and he was completely unready for life on the outside. His sole preoccupation was to clean out the jail's rubbish bins. That was his job and nothing else occupied his day except his obsessive bin cleaning. No rehabilitation, no courses and no leaves. To say the Batsman was not ready for release is an understatement.

The poor old Batsman had undertaken a basic cookery class in jail and had worked in the kitchen at Pentridge, he believed he was a "Silver Service Chef", whatever that may be! At every turn he would tell you, usually incorrectly, how to cook a particular dish.

I have always been a bit of a cook and once I arrived in the cottages at Fulham and was able to do some proper cooking I got right into it. The weekends were the highlight of my existence because that was when visits were allowed. I was very lucky that not one weekend went by without one of my friends making the trek from Melbourne all the way to Sale. Sale has nothing to recommend it, so those who visited did so purely out of friendship and not to take in the local sights.

I became a bit of a dab hand with cake cooking and I used to cook most of the week in eager anticipation of my visitors. We were allowed to take food out to the visit but unconsumed food could not go back to the unit. Visitors were not allowed to take away any food either. Leon Woods, one of the screws, would not even let my son take a muffin I had baked for his birthday out of the jail. The look of disappointment on my son's face tore my heart out. A good bloke is Mr Woods.

LUNATIC SOUP

One night I was baking a Lumber Jack cake for a visit and the Batsman was watching. I told him what I was baking and he observed that there was a lot of desecrated coconut in the recipe. I could not believe what he had just said, so I corrected him, telling him the coconut was desiccated, not desecrated – but no, Bob wanted to argue the toss. In exasperation I finally told him not to argue with me when it comes to the English language because desiccated means dried (and in this case shredded), while desecrated was what he did to mum and dad in the ute when he killed them! He did not get the joke!

Another Batsman story: Bob would use every dish, saucepan and utensil in the joint to make one small pizza base. One day I walked into the kitchen and there was stuff everywhere: on the benches, on the floor and on the stove. I asked whether Bob had caught "that bloke", to which he replied "Which bloke?" I said "The one who threw the hand grenade in the kitchen." Again he did not get the joke.

The fourth ex-serviceman in for a murder was Frank Garner, who also lived in my cottage at Fulham. How's that for the daily double: living with two blokes, both off their cruets and both convicted of indiscriminate murders! Garner had been involved in what he perceived as a matrimonial slight from his ex-wife and had gone around and blown his ex-wife's boyfriend away through a closed door. In other words, shot the wrong person and so then had tried to kill his ex-wife as well. I lived with Garner for over a year.

Norrie and Pickford had blocked their crimes out of their memories, so much so that they didn't think that they had committed any offence. Garner came from the other direction, was totally unrepentant and said he would do it all over again if the opportunity presented itself. Now that he has been released, one wonders what benefit he has had from being in prison. I worked with him in the laundry. Andrew Norrie cleaned cells at Port Phillip until he was deported. He undertook no programs, and in fact did nothing for himself, that would ready him for the outside world. Bob Pickford cleaned rubbish bins at Fulham until he was released. What a ripping effort in the rehab department!

What is going on in our armed forces if these types of people are accepted into the armed services when they are clearly not mentally stable? Is it the army that fails to address the issue or discover the problem while recruiting, or does the army make these people that way? Whichever way it goes, it is a disturbing trend.

The second and more unsettling aspect is that not one of these men, as far as I could see, received any treatment at all that dealt with the matter of their extraordinarily violent offending. All four men had served, or are serving, big sentences and were to be released back into the community without any adequate preparation for what I personally found a confronting return to the real world. If I felt so confronted re-entering the community after five years how must have these blokes have felt after a double figure whack?

Nobody seems to ask these questions and most assuredly the Office of Corrections volunteers no answer. It further raises the question: What in God's name is the Parole Board doing? It is well known in prison that there are certain answers the Parole Board seeks when interviewing a prisoner and if you answer correctly your parole chances are greatly enhanced. These blokes finish their sentences and they are let out the door. They are let out the door without any preparation for the outside world and if they can't cope out there, the obvious reaction is that they are likely to kill again.

By the way, I never got to see the Parole Board. I was released without once seeing anybody from Parole or discussing the matter of parole with anybody. I was on the list to see the Parole Board before I left jail but my name was taken off the list without any explanation whatsoever. The only thing I received from the Parole Board, to ready me for the outside world, was a discussion with the officer at Fulham whose job it was to prepare you for the outside world by "helping" you with opening bank accounts, getting on the dole, and filling out various other forms. I went down and sat with him and filled out all the necessary paperwork. The next day he told me he had been in to Sale and lodged everything, so when I was released I would automatically be on the dole and a bank account would be open. Wrong! When I was released from jail I attended the dole office with a piece of paper that this officer had given me. I presented it and the dole officer looked up the computer only to find nothing had been lodged. The result was hours at Centrelink filling out forms that I'd been told had already been completed and lodged on my behalf. This is the help you get in jail to make your transition back into the real world as seamless and stress free as possible.

Chapter 4
Peter Dupas: The Story So Far

Ah! Well a day!
What evil looks
Had I from old and young!
Instead of the cross,
the albatross
About my neck was hung.

– SAMUEL TAYLOR COLERIDGE, *RIME OF THE ANCIENT MARINER*

Standing at muster on my first night in Sirius East, having looked around and seen all the detritus of humanity that I was banged up with, I shuddered. I shuddered when I thought of the horrific crimes and the awful suffering this group of men had brought upon society. But none sent a shudder down my spine more than the small, fat, bespectacled, baby-faced man standing directly opposite me staring blankly into space. That man was Peter Norris Dupas.

Outwardly Dupas looks innocence personified: straight hair that never stays combed away from a fringe for longer than a moment and which flops down over his forehead. To give the hairstyle an innocent name from my youth, he sported a Beatle Cut. Large thick spectacles, a round pudgy face to match his short pudgy body, he rather reminded me of Pugsley in the 1960s TV show *The Addams Family*. But what you see is not always what you get. I knew from my life as a criminal lawyer that Dupas had a long and extensive criminal history, all for violent sexually related offences. When I first met him, this career of perennial sexual offending had culminated in his being sentenced to a life sentence with no minimum term being set for the mutilation murder of a psychologist, Nicole Patterson, in her consulting suite attached to her home. Her murder was particularly violent and gruesome, and the actions in this murder completely belied the looks of Dupas. However, I was to find out over the next fifteen months what a seething mass of psychopathic pathology this man really was.

The real question is: How, over all of the years of Dupas's sexual offending, was he allowed time and again to be back on the street or time and again to be released unsupervised, only to reoffend? On some occasions, as you will see, he offended time and again over the space of a couple of weeks, yet never, ever was he found to be a serious sexual offender, which would have enabled a court to sentence him to an indefinite term of imprisonment without parole.

Being a defence lawyer and a court room smarty pants is all well and good, except when society is genuinely being put at risk. When Dupas was sentenced for the last offence before the murders of Nicole Patterson, Margaret Maher and Mersina Halvagis, he was in the gun to be sentenced as a serious sexual offender. But the joint efforts of the prosecution and the defence led the judge to not sentence Dupas to an indefinite term of imprisonment. I really wonder how the barrister appearing on his behalf on that occasion – being from Legal Aid, which is funded by you and me, the taxpayers – and the prosecutor live with themselves. I wonder if it ever crosses their minds in the dark depths of night that they are partially responsible for the death of these three innocent women. More importantly, what about the presiding judge? On reading the reports of these proceedings I see that it was one and the same judge who sentenced me years later, Judge Leo Hart.

Peter Dupas was born in Sydney on 6 July 1953, the youngest of three children. His parents moved to Melbourne while he was still a baby. At fifteen years of age, Dupas first manifested his violent disposition towards women when, on 3 October 1968, he visited unannounced the house next door to where he was living in Melbourne's Mount Waverley and asked the single mother whether he could borrow a kitchen knife as little Peter was helping peel the vegies for the evening's dinner. Not surprisingly, Dupas's first victim thought "What a nice boy, he is helping his mum." Julie went to the kitchen and gave him a knife, whereupon Dupas, without warning, attacked Julie and started stabbing her over and over. He knocked her to the ground and ended up on top of her. Dupas then started crying, saying "I can't stop, I can't stop." This was an extraordinary outburst from such a young offender and he was duly sentenced in the Children's Court to eighteen months' probation and sent to a psychiatric hospital for examination.

Note the obvious power of this attack when a fifteen-year-old boy easily overpowers a grown woman. This attack was a precursor of things to come. Every alarm bell in creation should have been ringing in that Children's Court, even back then.

You will love this: have a guess how many times Dupas saw the psychiatrist for psychiatric evaluation after such an extraordinary, unannounced, gratuitous and violent assault. Once! Yes, he saw a psychiatrist once. That was the extent of his supervision over eighteen months while subject to a probation order.

For many years, as a defence lawyer, when I couldn't avoid it, I appeared in the Children's Court. The attitude of the magistrates in the Children's Court is one of benevolence. Time and again little Johnny reappears before the Court having offended again, and once again the child is released on a bond to be of good behaviour for a given period of time, notwithstanding the fact that they have often breached a previous bond or bonds. In extreme cases, the young offender is placed on probation. Probation, while it is ordered to be supervised, is in fact unsupervised. By definition, probation is supervised; but such is the state of the system that probation is nothing more than window dressing.

I should know. I have experienced the joys of supervision by the parole board personally and can say that parole has done absolutely nothing for me and on occasions has actually placed impediments in the way of my rehabilitation. Here are a couple of examples. When *Court in the Middle* was published, it was arranged for me to be interviewed on *Enough Rope* on the ABC, the highest rating TV interview show in the country. To be interviewed I had to travel to Sydney. I should say the ticket was paid for by my publishers and I was to be travelling up and back on the same day with my manager and a publicist.

I was told, to my amazement, that my request to travel would probably be denied. I was staggered. This was the launch of my new life. On my next visit I told my parole officer that I would certainly sell more books if permission to travel was refused. Why? "Because I will pillory you in the media." To which came the reply, "But it won't be my decision." I replied: "You will be the one conveying the decision to me." About an hour later I was telephoned and told I was allowed to travel.

The second and more surprising example was when I applied for a state government clearance to work with children. I had been working with a Melbourne charity,

Open Family, speaking in schools to kids about the dangers of drug use and how drugs can bring anyone down. One would have thought that these talks were of enormous relevance to kids and of real community benefit, so an application was made for a clearance. I attended Parole and my parole officer advised that, while he supported my application, his superiors opposed it. No reason given – just opposed. Fortunately the police could see the value of this contribution and supported my application, which has since been granted after an eighteen-month delay. No thanks to the Office of Corrections!

Back in the Children's Court, kids very quickly wake up to the fact that you can go back to court again and again until you are blue in the face and you will at worst receive a slap over the wrist from some caring and sharing magistrate. Only in the most extreme cases will a juvenile offender be sent to what is oxymoronically referred to as a Youth Training Centre. At YTC the youth is supposed to be taught appropriate skills to cope in society, without reoffending, after release. How is it, then, that the majority of the young blokes I have seen over the years, both in and out of the nick, who have had stints at these so called YTCs are illiterate? Once again there is no explanation. Society ought be outraged. By the way, it is a human rights violation not to offer education in a place of detention.

We live in a society and are required to live by its rules, irrespective of our age. If we don't abide by society's rules, we should be sanctioned, and sanctioned in a manner that makes us think twice about reoffending. The present regime in the Children's Court is such that kids don't get that message. I've appeared for kids who have stabbed people at parties and they receive a good behaviour bond. These kids should be subject to stringent sanctions that see them properly supervised and *educated*. They should be required to do something of benefit for the community by putting something back into that community. Good behaviour bonds must be changed to mean more than just that. Otherwise, it's as the criminals say – "sign the sorry book" and head off into the sunset with the overwhelming feeling that you have committed an offence with impunity and can do so again. The Children's Court is a paper tiger.

The natural extension of this regime is that a child offender who continues to offend until they reach adult court age will eventually front court and be somewhat stunned to find out that the presiding judge or magistrate takes a very dim view of their very lengthy history of anti-social behaviour and they finally end up in jail. Of course, jail is merely an advanced college of criminal education, in the practical sense, and you come out worse than when you went in.

I have made this complaint before and I will continue to make it until somebody takes notice and puts an end to this idiocy.

If, as an ordinary member of the public, you sat in the Children's Court for a day and saw the categories of offences that are committed – particularly car theft and offences of a similar nature, such as burglary, where your home has been invaded and your valuables are stolen – and saw the manner in which the children are "reprimanded", you would be horrified.

No doubt the signal, this disposition, sent to the fifteen-year-old Peter Dupas was similar. He could reoffend with impunity, and did so time and again over many years until he finally brought himself undone. What would have been the case if Peter junior had been jumped on from a great height when a pattern first emerged in his offending.

I remember talking to a senior police officer one day at the Children's Court. He was there because there had been a very serious assault and I was appearing for the accused, but there had also been a complaint made by that kid and his parents about police treatment. During the conversation I asked him why there were so many kids being charged and processed by the Children's Court these days. I found his answer very interesting.

Once upon a time, in the good old days, if young Johnny was caught breaking windows or playing up in the street and fighting, the coppers would get hold of him and (quote) "give them a good foot up the arse and send them home". If that had happened to me as a young kid, I would not have gone home and told my old man what I had been up to in a million years. I wouldn't have done it because Dad's very first question would have been: What were you doing to deserve a foot in the arse from the coppers? Instead, what this senior officer told me was that the kids go home and say "I have been assaulted by the police" and the parents immediately jump to the wrong conclusion and think they have a problem with the police. They don't stop and take stock of what the child has been up to in order to earn that foot in the arse. Rather, these days, by making an allegation of police brutality the kid slips off the hook without being dealt with properly. Such is the idiotic state of our society.

On 10 March 1972, young Peter Dupas was caught peeping at a woman through the window of her Oakleigh home. He already had a conviction for stabbing another woman multiple times and in such horrific circumstances, so it would have been reasonable to assume that he might have been planning to behave in that way again. He received a fifty dollar fine.

What happens next is illustrative of my argument that people like Dupas should be dealt with swiftly and early. On 5 November 1973, he rapes a woman in Mitcham at knifepoint and threatens her baby. No one in their right mind would threaten a child but it's indicative of the type of person Dupas is.

Ten days later, Dupas is questioned again by police after frightening a twelve-year-old girl by following her and repeatedly staring at her. This staring aspect raises its head again and again in his behaviour and is one of the reasons he could be identified as being at Fawkner Cemetery on the day of the murder of Mersina Halvagis. It is a cold, calculating, unblinking stare that I have personally witnessed on a number of occasions and let me tell you, even for a bloke it is very unnerving indeed!

A mere fifteen days later, on 30 November 1973, Dupas is charged with the rape and in addition also cops charges of house breaking, stealing and house breaking with intent to commit a felony. This warped kid has become a one-man sexually driven crime wave and is still only twenty years old. He has already chalked up three different sets of sexually related offences. The alarm bells should have been well and truly ringing by now, but the powers that be appear to suffer industrial deafness!

Then, still not twenty-one, and while on bail for all of the other offences committed in November 1973, Dupas is remanded to a psychiatric hospital for peeping at young girls showering in a toilet block at Rosebud beach. He is fined the princely sum of $140 for an attempt to commit a felony and offensive behaviour.

How long did Dupas spend in that psychiatric hospital? One day! By the time he has spent his one day in a psychiatric hospital he has committed no fewer than five sexually violent offences or sexual offences. He is remanded in custody at that stage for the previous bail-related offences but he has still only spent one day in psychiatric care. It appears that he did not receive any other psychiatric counselling or treatment during that period yet his violent sexual behaviour was far from normal.

The long arm of the law finally catches up Dupas on 30 September 1974, just after his twenty-first birthday and he is jailed for nine years with a minimum of five.

Dupas completed his five-year minimum for the 1973 rape and was released on 4 September 1979. With the remainder of his nine-year term to be served on parole, he was subject to Parole Board supervision for the outstanding four years. This meant that they were supposed to look after him and assist with his re-integration into the community and with his rehabilitation.

Every red light possible should have been flashing when Dupas was released. I can say from personal experience that the Parole Board does absolutely nothing to assist in your re-integration into society or with your rehabilitation. In the twenty-month period up to the writing of this book, I have had four parole officers assigned to me, none of whom has been able to assist me in any way. I have been asked countless brainless questions such as, "How's it going? or "Has anything changed?" Nobody can explain to me what "Has anything changed?" means. Have I changed my mind, my socks, my diet, my attitude? If they could explain, then I'd be only too happy to answer the question.

The only other thing they do is occasionally send you off for a random urine sample at Dorovich Pathology, where you are met by people who clearly hate the fact that they have to take urine samples from – as one Dorovich employee put it to me – "junkies". (As I had at that stage been clean for seven years, I took extreme exception to this.) I was also told that I could not give a sample in the morning – that time is reserved for people who work. Instead, the afternoons were when "your type" attended. I hit the roof and told the woman that she was discriminating against me and was wrongly supposing that I did not work and that I still used. I refused to move until my sample was taken, which reluctantly happened. How do people fare who cannot stick up for themselves like I did?

So young Peter is released on parole. He is living in the southern bayside suburb of Frankston when, on 9 November 1979, he rapes a woman, again wielding a knife. He has been out two months and he is on parole. Two days later, on 11 November, he chases a woman with a knife but she runs away. Lucky for her. Seven days later, on 18 November, out of the blue Dupas attacks and stabs an elderly woman in the chest. He makes a run for it and gets away. The very next day Dupas tries to grab a Frankton woman and abduct her. She screams and he bolts. This offending, all committed in Frankston, is becoming repetitious, isn't it?

Between his release on 4 September and 19 November 1979, a period of ten weeks, he commits no fewer than four sexually related assaults, all in the same area, two of them with knives, against single women. Has it crossed anybody's mind yet that there's a pretty clear pattern emerging in this bloke's offences and that he is extraordinarily dangerous? Finally he is arrested, bail is refused and he is held on remand pending trial.

On 2 June 1980 he is sentenced to six years with a minimum of five years for the Frankston offences. What about his unfinished parole? He should be serving the unexpired portion of his parole as well as any penalty for the breach of his parole, in addition to the sentence received for the Frankston offences. On my calculations this adds up to a ten-year minimum sentence to serve. That he got half of this needs to be explained.

Significantly, because Dupas's sentence was of a period of more than three years, he was entitled to temporary release from jail before his release on parole. The idea of temporary release is to help people get ready for re-entry into society. For eight days from 6 to 14 February 1985, Dupas is allowed pre-release from jail. Then, on 27 February 1985, he is finally released from jail, on parole, again.

Four days later, Dupas rapes a 21-year-old woman at Blairgowrie back beach. This time the courts are a little quicker in dealing with him because he pleads Guilty. On 28 June 1985 Dupas is sentenced to twelve years' imprisonment with a minimum of ten years. However, he is released on parole in March 1992 after having served less than seven years of a ten-year minimum. Don't forget that, all along the way, unexpired portions of parole are accumulating, including the five years he was currently completing on parole. It is not clear from his history precisely what has happened to all those unexpired periods of parole, save to say that he doesn't seem to have ever served them.

After Dupas's release on this occasion it takes a little longer for him to start reoffending – a whole eighteen months. As far as we know! The inevitable happens on 23 September 1993, when he attempts to assault a girl while she is horse-riding at Kyneton. Don't forget that this is a man who has now been in and out of jail since October of 1968 and we are now at September 1993. Over this extended period of time Dupas has repeatedly and violently offended, but on this occasion the Director of Public Prosecutions does not authorise a prosecution for these offences and again the system fails to protect the community. Why was he not breached on his parole and sent back to jail? I would love to know.

Once again patterns continue to emerge. On 5 November 1993, less than two months after the attempted assault at Kyneton, Renita Brunton is murdered and stabbed up to 106 times in her Sunbury shop. I often wondered how difficult it would be to stab somebody more than a hundred times in a short space of time with the amount of strength required. The reader should pick up a knife and just try stabbing the air ten or twenty times and see how hard that is on your arm. To punch a sharp knife into a human body a hundred times must require super-human strength, obviously brought about by some adrenaline driven frenzy. (This sort of strength would be demonstrated to me later by Dupas.) Brunton's murder remains unsolved and I understand that Dupas is the only suspect for it. The pattern from all of his offending is that he picks women who are alone so that he feels in control of the situation. If he feels that way then he will attack and, given the opportunity, kill – but not just kill, mutilate in what's clearly a frenzy. If he feels like he might be caught, he goes elsewhere for his next victim. This murder is typical of Dupas in that she was a woman on her own – there were no males within the immediate vicinity.

Two months later, on 3 January 1994, Dupas goes to Lake Epaloch. Lake Epaloch is a water storage area in the general vicinity of Woodend. Woodend, Kyneton, Sunbury, all north-west of Melbourne ... see the pattern emerging yet again? He attacks a woman in the toilet block and indecently assaults her.

The next part leaves me speechless with its ineptitude by the courts and the barristers, who are after all, officers of the court. Dupas is charged over the attack on 3 January and he pleads Guilty on 21 November 1994. His barrister does a deal with the prosecution and Dupas is jailed for three years and nine months for false imprisonment. At this stage Dupas is well and truly in the frame for an indefinite sentence under the dangerous offender's legislation. This is not raised by the prosecution nor are the many years of unserved parole and Dupas again crawls through the cracks of a system that is fundamentally flawed in its inability to protect you and me against such offenders.

Three years and nine months for a count of false imprisonment is a straight sentence with no parole involved. Three years and nine months from 21 November 1994 would take you to August 1998. Why he is released on 29 September 1996, I do not know. No one from Corrections has ever volunteered an explanation and I doubt they will ever do so because to do so would leave someone's arse hanging out in the breeze!

Ten months after Dupas walks from jail, on 4 October 1997 Margaret Maher's body is found dumped near the Hume Freeway at Somerton. Dupas will later be convicted of her murder and sentenced to life with no minimum. But meanwhile, on 1 November 1997, less than a month after Margaret Maher's murder, Mersina Halvagis is stabbed to death at the Fawkner Cemetery in Melbourne while visiting her grandmother's grave – a most shocking crime. After Mersina's death, there is a bit of a break for a couple of months, until 30 December 1997, when Kathleen Downs, a 95-year-old widow, is found stabbed to death in a Brunswick nursing home. Dupas is the only suspect for this murder but has never been charged.

But Dupas is still a free man and on 19 April 1999, Nicole Patterson, a psychologist, is murdered at her home, where she also ran her consulting suite. Once again the attack was a frenzied knife attack with a severe blow to the side of the head and both of the victims breasts removed. The pattern is well and truly set: Margaret Maher, Mersina Halvagis,

Kathleen Downs and Nicole Patterson all murdered in similar circumstances, with a concentration of stab wounds around the chest area and the Dupas signature of a slash to the inner thigh of each of the deceased. Interestingly enough there was also a previous break-in at the mortuary at the Austin Hospital in 1969, when the bodies of two elderly women were mutilated in a similar way, also with a very sharp knife.

From my experience as a criminal lawyer, serial killers or recidivists of just about any nature, even including armed robbers, have a signature in the way they offend. If it's an armed robber they may use a similar disguise, they may use a similar type of car to drive away from the scene or use a similar type of weapon or say similar things. No matter what it is, patterns invariably emerge if you study a series of cases closely enough. The murders Dupas committed were no exception. They were all violent to the point of being frenzied. The stab wounds were concentrated on the chest area and there was a slash on the inner thigh and a severe blow with a blunt instrument to the side of the head. If that's not a signature of a serial killer, I don't know what is.

On 15 August 2000, Dupas pleads Not Guilty to the murder of Nicole Patterson and is convicted by a Supreme Court jury. He is *finally* sentenced to life with no minimum.

This is not the end, however. The police are so horrified with Dupas's behaviour and so fixated on the clear pattern of offending, that a task force called Micardo is set up to investigate him further in relation to other unsolved murders. This is where I come in, but first let me finish the chronology.

On 2 October 2000, while serving one life sentence with no minimum, Dupas is charged with the murder of Margaret Maher. Breathtakingly, though, despite the presence of DNA evidence at the scene linking Dupas to that crime, a learned (and I use that word advisedly) magistrate refuses to commit Dupas to stand trial after a committal hearing. Fortunately the Director of Public Prosecutions, Paul Coghlan QC (now Mr Justice Coghlan of the Supreme Court of Victoria) presents him directly to the Supreme Court. It was a good call because one year later, after a lengthy trial in which Dupas once again has pleaded Not Guilty, he is convicted of the murder of Margaret Maher. Dupas is sentenced for a second time to a term of life imprisonment with no minimum.

After my release on 11 September 2006 and having made my formal statement to the police regarding Halvagis on the same day, Dupas is taken from jail without warning directly to the Supreme Court where he is charged with the murder of Mersina Halvagis. This charge is laid by means of what is called a direct presentment. With a direct presentment the Director of Public Prosecutions elects not to have the matter dragged through the Magistrate's Court again by way of committal proceedings and instead asks a Supreme Court judge to deal with the matter from the word go.

The eleven months leading up to 9 August 2007, when Dupas was finally found guilty of murdering Mersina

LUNATIC SOUP

Halvagis, were long and arduous for me. The verdict came
after a lengthy trial where he pleaded – you guessed it – Not
Guilty. He is now serving three life sentences without a
minimum and will never be released back into society.

That is still not the end of the story. The police continue
to investigate Dupas for some of the other unsolved murders
that I have mentioned.

As you read this extraordinary criminal history one thing
jumps out at you time and again, and that is the complete
failure of the court system to protect precisely those they are
there to protect – you, me, the general public. Dupas was
released early time and again after having breached his
parole. The normal position is that if you are released on
parole and you breach that parole, it is cancelled and you go
straight back into custody and start serving the unexpired
portion of your parole. When you then go to court over the
charges that you breached your parole, you can be sentenced
to an additional term of imprisonment for the breach, on top
of the remaining original term.

In the case of Dupas, it is apparent that no treatment was
given to this man while he was in jail – and I have witnessed
that with my own eyes. Occasionally a pastoral worker came
in and talked to him, and apart from that he took medication
that would stop a herd of stampeding elephants in its tracks.
That was while he was serving three life sentences. He clearly
wasn't that restrained when he wasn't on medication and he
was released into the community. What treatment was

afforded Dupas at that time, and how effective it was, no one is saying. Nobody has revealed what medication he was on, if any; what supervision he was subjected to, if any. When these questions are asked of the Parole Board, the Corrections Commissioner, the politicians involved, everybody ducks for cover and does the usual trick of keeping their head down and hoping like hell it will all go away. Sooner or later somebody is actually going to ask them to account for their lack of action and to respond to the allegation that, by their omissions, they knowingly exposed the community to increased danger. I will be among the first to level this allegation because if you think for one moment that Dupas is the only person who is capable of committing these sorts of offences, then you are sadly mistaken. I lived with thirty-seven of these blokes for fifteen months and it is not pleasant. Many, but not all, are never to be released and can never be rehabilitated. They lack any remorse, are even proud of what they have done and often sit around skiting about their crimes.

Chapter 5

Living Next Door to Peter

The evil men do lives after them: the good is oft
interred with their bones.

– WILLIAM SHAKESPEARE, *JULIUS CAESAR*

Standing there on muster on my first night in Sirius East,
it strikes me that nothing could be blacker. Somehow I
have ended up in a unit of thirty-eight blokes: thirty-
seven psychopaths and me. It soon becomes apparent to
me that Andrew Davies, my new cell mate, is despised by
all the members of the unit with the exception of the
other paedophiles. Rock spiders carry no weight in jail;
they are despised. Most of the rock spiders spend their
time as cave dwellers – that is, blokes who sit in their
cells all day with the curtains drawn and the door closed.
There they sit chain smoking and watching television for
the entirety of their sentence. If that's what they want to

do that's what the screws let them do – it keeps them quiet.

The person facing me, however, was different. Peter Dupas had killed and killed often. But standing there was an insignificant, pudgy-looking man, motionless, as still as a sphinx except for his eyes which darted everywhere. He had a brooding, calculating malevolence about him. He oozed passive aggression. He was clearly somebody to keep a very close eye on, as time would soon tell.

Even on that cursory first glance, it was apparent that Dupas stood apart from the others in the unit, notwithstanding their collectively horrific crimes. There was something about him that made him different and in my first couple of months in the unit I was to find out what.

Jail is really pretty simple. There are three rules: see no evil, hear no evil and speak no evil – the three wise monkeys are alive and well. You particularly do not ask what somebody is "in" for. Being considered prying or nosey invites violence and I have seen that first hand. Also, serving huge sentences, like virtually everybody in Sirius East, makes people paranoid. Jail thinking is completely different to the thinking of the normal community. People see a conspiracy around every corner and see a police informer under every blade of grass.

One day when I had been moved out of protection and into mainstream I was in the same unit as a bloke called Liam Bernie, who was being given a trial run in mainstream to see if he could cope. Bernie had committed an armed robbery at a Kmart store and, while driving the getaway car through the car park, ran over an old lady. Most normal human beings would stop to render assistance. Not Liam. He got out, looked at her lying prone on the ground and then got back in the car and backed over her to make sure she was dead.

At the time when Bernie and I crossed paths, there was a huge amount of publicity about prisoners being able to ring the Crime Stoppers telephone number without charge and with supposedly total anonymity, which is bulldust because every telephone call is monitored. But we were all encouraged to ring Crime Stoppers and lag our little hearts out. Needless to say, this initiative was the talk of the jail. One morning I was sitting reading the paper in the library. Liam was there and I jokingly said to him that we'd all better get on the phone quick smart – clearly meant to be a joke. He got up and stormed out. Some time later that morning I was in my cell reading a book when the door was slammed shut. I looked up and there was Bernie. His eyes were nearly out on stalks with rage. He has no front teeth, he is covered in jail tattoos from head to foot, is fat but very strong – and to say that he is a loose canon would be an understatement. He came and stood over me as I was sitting on a chair and screamed abuse at me about suggesting he was a police informer. He said that's the sort of thing that could get me killed or, if the wrong bloke heard it, get him killed. The tirade went on for some minutes, and that is a very long time in the company of someone like Bernie. I was in real fear of being severely bashed or worse. I kept telling him that it was meant to be a joke and that I had used the word *we* instead of the word *you* when I talked about jumping on the phone. This did absolutely nothing to placate him and he kept screaming and shouting until I finally talked him into leaving my cell when I promised I wouldn't talk to him again. This is what you face in jail: irrational crazed outbursts by people whose medication probably isn't agreeing with them.

Not Peter Dupas, though – quiet, sneaking around, desperately trying to keep under the radar, everybody giving him a wide berth. After effectively not talking to anybody except my cell mate for the first couple of weeks and at the same time sitting back observing life in the unit, it became apparent to me that Dupas was the head of one of the two factions in the unit. As I said, a lot of the blokes in the unit are cave dwellers and don't get involved in the internal politics at all. They are too terrified. However, Dupas, Ray Edmunds (Mr Stinky), Paul Gorman, Andrew Norrie and Biff were all in the Dupas crew and Les Camilleri and Christopher Hall and other assorted dead beats made up the other crew. They all had a real John Howard attitude to life – you are either with us or against us; there are no half measures – so having witnessed a stabbing in the food queue after I had only been there a couple of days I decided it was probably best not to try to make friends with anybody, and if anybody was interested in talking to me they could come to me.

While not a daily occurrence, such stabbings were regular and there are plenty of blokes wandering around the jail system with more holes than a Swiss cheese, proudly mouthing off about how many times they have been shivved. Typically a number of fast blows were delivered with lightning speed, preferably to the neck or to the head. All hell would then break loose and a huge fight ensue, with the screws standing back and watching the excitement and letting the fight punch itself to a standstill. Then the screws would move in, call the riot squad and lock the unit down. The perpetrators would be taken away to hospital or to the slot.

Prison life affects people. They are without hope and have nothing but the boredom of prison life to look forward to. Your every movement is monitored. You are told when to get up, when to shower, when to eat and when to shit. It's stifling, suppressive and depressing. Blokes who are doing life have nothing to look forward to so the unimportant becomes life and death to them. Who gives a bugger if you are first or last in the queue for your meal? They do. Things that don't matter in the real world are blown out of all proportion. I've seen blokes bashed over a can of coke and stabbed over a pouch of tobacco. On the outside they wouldn't bother. All these blokes see are walls for the rest of their lives. You have a volatile situation where they have nothing materially and so they have nothing to lose.

Dupas didn't get himself involved in any of these fights. He didn't need to. He was quiet, secretive, calculating and bloody dangerous. I would go as far as to say that he is probably the most dangerous person I have ever met – and that is really saying something, having been a criminal defence lawyer for over twenty-eight years and having acted for many murderers and other violent offenders or people just plain off their nuts.

Dupas always sat at a particular spot to eat his meals and he always ate with Ray Edmunds and Paul Gorman. You didn't dare sit at that table unless invited. Camilleri and his crew ate at another table on the other side of the unit and the cave dwellers usually grabbed their meals and scuttled back to their cells as quickly as they could.

Dupas did not actively seek anybody's company; rather, people sought him out obviously as a protection move. Camilleri was the exact opposite. He was a large man. He was loud. He had a real "look at me" attitude and spat the dummy whenever something didn't go his way. Camilleri wanted to enlist blokes into his crew because, when it came to the power base within the unit, they were severely undermanned.

For the first couple of weeks in the unit I said nothing to Dupas – we just made a nodding acknowledgment of each other whenever we made eye contact. It was in fact Ray Edmunds who first spoke to me and introduced himself, but he needed no introduction as I well and truly knew who he

was and the despicable crimes he had been convicted of.
Then, one day while walking back to my cell with my lunch,
I had to walk past Dupas's table on my way. He looked up
and said "Hey, Andrew, why don't you sit here and join us?"
At that time only Edmunds and Dupas were sitting at the
table. I'd already made a calculated judgment that the Dupas
crew was far stronger than Camilleri's and when I was invited
I thought I might as well get with the strength – it might at
some stage come in handy if the shit did hit the fan with
Camilleri. I sat down. Dupas formally introduced himself
and we chatted about nothing in particular. That was the
start of the ride that was going to take me into the Supreme
Court of Victoria in July 2007 when I was to give evidence
against Peter Dupas in his trial for the murder of Mersina
Halvagis.

In Sirius East there is a garden area and within that is a
vegetable patch. Dupas's only passion in life was this vegie
patch. He would head out there to spend every available
moment that he was allowed. He was the unit gardener,
assisted by a Chinese prisoner who was in for trafficking huge
amounts of heroin and blowing the proceeds at Crown
Casino. My cell had a view of this garden and I used to sit
and watch the two at work out there. The Chinese bloke
was in protection because it was perceived in the jail
community that he had a lot of money. Common sense plays
no part in the thought processes in jail. What prisoners knew
was that this man had lost a lot of money gambling at Crown

Casino. It illogically follows in jail that, if he had that much cash to blow at the Casino, he must still have a large amount which could be scared out of him. The reality was that this bloke's assets had been seized under Proceeds of Crimes legislation, so he was effectively penniless. However, he had been hassled so much in mainstream for money that he had to be put in protection.

Dupas would get very anxious if he couldn't get out into the garden for some security reason or if he was denied anything for the garden, which regularly happened. To give you an idea of the rehabilitation deliberately withheld in prison, even though we had a vegetable garden it was virtually impossible to obtain seeds. My sister was prepared to pay for some packets of vegetable seeds to be sent in to the jail via the horticultural teacher so we could have something to grow, but her offer was declined. So we saved the seeds out of tomatoes, capsicums and chillies. Dupas would painstakingly remove the seeds and fastidiously dry them on toilet paper on his window sill. He would then sort them and plant them the next season. That was how we got our seeds.

Dupas continued in the garden and I continued doing nuts and bolts. At the end of each afternoon, the nuts and bolts workroom was left empty – no more screaming and shouting or smoke-filled air. It was deserted, quiet, relatively fresh and somewhere you could be somewhat at peace.

By the way, although smoking is banned just about everywhere in this country now, it is still permitted in jails.

LUNATIC SOUP

At Sirius East the common areas of the unit were the only places you were not allowed to smoke. One senior officer once said to me that jails run on nicotine and caffeine and it is just too hard to stop both the inmates and the screws from smoking. Each cell is full of cigarette smoke, which obviously permeates the entire unit. People also smoke outside and they smoke in the workroom. So to be able to go out to the workroom after hours and sit there in a smoke-free environment was, for somebody like me who has never smoked in his life, a blessing.

One afternoon I was sitting out in the workroom, facing the door, quietly doing nuts and bolts – lost in my thoughts, lamenting the disastrous state of my life – when Edmunds, Gorman and Dupas all wandered in over a span of a few minutes and sat down to do nuts and bolts too. At that stage I didn't socialise with anybody in the unit. I'd only been in jail a relatively short period compared with these blokes, who had done well over fifteen years each, and I didn't want to sound like I was whinging. In jail, if you have a short sentence and you complain about it to a long-termer, you are told in no uncertain terms that you copped a "drunk's lagging" and to kick along with it and stop whinging. The origin of this expression is that anyone charged with drunk and disorderly is locked up for four hours until they are sober and then they are discharged without conviction.

As a distraction from the mind-numbing activity of assembling Dynabolts, we all started talking about our respective crimes. This was the first time I'd had any discussion with any of these blokes about their offences and I was somewhat apprehensive, but, like anybody, I had a morbid fascination for what they would have to say about themselves. I stuck my hand up first, saying that I had pleaded Guilty and therefore I was guilty of what the Crown had alleged. It would have been most unwise, at that stage, to express any other view of my own culpability.

Ray Edmunds volunteered that he had committed some terrible crimes and reckoned he had paid a hefty penalty for them. He was still paying that penalty, as he had been in jail over twenty years. He said he regretted what he had done. Frankly that didn't carry much weight with me because Edmunds was now around seventy and his crimes were serial rapes and murders carried out in the most audacious manner over some years. He was clearly a recidivist who, if given the chance to be back in the community, would probably reoffend despite his advanced years.

Paul Gorman, chatting along with us, had served well in excess of ten years and was still unrepentant: he boasted that he would get out and reoffend in a very short space of time. As an example of the duty of care *not* shown by the authorities, this was the man who always volunteered to share a cell with young blokes sent to protection precisely *because* they were young and vulnerable and had malleable personalities. He would do this under the guise of helping them through a difficult period – and guess what would happen! Within a couple of days, the young bloke had been moved because he had made complaints against Gorman for unwarranted sexual advances and in some cases sexual assault. All that happened was that these blokes were moved. I understand Gorman was subsequently convicted of a jail rape and had an extra few months added to his sentence. He once said to me, in a group, it doesn't matter where you put "it" as long as it's out of sight – at which we all laughed. Now I am home, away from the jail atmosphere, I find that type of comment disgusting in the extreme.

The other person at the table on this day, Peter Dupas, sat on my right, fiddling with the nuts and bolts and just staring at the table. I can still see him now. Edmunds said, "What about you, Pete? Spit it out." Dupas continued to look at the table. Then he said words to the effect that "I've been convicted so I've got to wear it." That was in relation to Nicole Patterson's murder only. No other matters had reared their ugly head at this stage, even though I knew full well that the police were investigating Dupas for further crimes and that he was a red-hot suspect in at least two and probably more murders.

Time drags in jail so I don't know how long it was after this that I applied for a job in the garden. I was told by the supervisor of the unit, Mr Fox, that he would consider my request but the other blokes had the job at the time and I would be a candidate for it only if one of them left. Surprisingly he asked me whether I would be able to work with Dupas. In every other job I had in jail, I was *told* what I would be doing, not asked, and I find it significant that this officer was so concerned about Dupas that he asked me whether I could work with him.

Time continued to drag. Eventually the Chinese prisoner was moved to a country jail in preparation for being deported, so I scored the gardening job. This was great because I could be outside more and actually have something to occupy my mind apart from staring at nuts and bolts. I also took the opportunity to enrol in a horticulture course, which was strictly elementary: I knew most of it, having been interested in gardening and particularly Australian native plants most of my life. However, we were given a couple of videos to watch and Dupas and I would watch them together, always in his cell, and we would have the horticulture teacher come occasionally to teach us stuff in the garden. With the rudimentary tools and few plants provided, together with the attitude of the authorities, the kind of gardening we could do was basic to say the least.

Dupas was obsessive – not just in the garden, but about himself and his cell, which was pristine. To give you an idea of just how obsessive he was, in jail it is very hard to get hold of any proper cleaning materials, but somehow Dupas had an entire bottle of floor polish and a scrubbing brush, a small paintbrush, about a two inch brush. Every morning after his shower, he would wipe out his shower recess, which was on the same level as the floor – it was all a poured concrete floor. Then, after let-out, everyday without fail he would paint his entire floor with floor polish. He would paint his way back towards the door and would then go outside to do his gardening and leave it to dry. Also, as a matter of protocol, you never, ever barged into Dupas's cell unannounced. If you did – and I saw this with my own eyes – he would stare, shake, and threaten you.

Swearing in jail is endemic. Everybody swears, non-stop. You become completely conditioned to it. However, the first time I heard Dupas utter the word *cunt* I was absolutely dumbfounded. It sent a shiver down my spine. He spat the word out with such venom that it made me stop in my tracks, realising how much he must hate women. I have never forgotten it. So when Dupas told you to fuck off he really meant it, and you did so and you did so smartly.

After polishing his floor every day Dupas would then put a towel on the floor. To visit him, you had to follow a procedure: you would go to his cell and knock on the door. Dupas would always be sitting on his bed watching television, his hands clasped between his knees, which later became significant. He would then look around and either he would say Yes, you could come in or he would tell you to fuck off. If you were invited in, and only if you were invited in, you then took off your shoes and stepped across the threshold onto the towel – whatever you do, don't step on the floor – and then sit at the end of his bed on the edge. That was it, that was his obsessive, controlling type of behaviour.

It might seem astounding, but we were allowed out into the garden on our own, with no supervision. Here was a man who was a serial killer, whose modus operandi was killing by repeated stabbings and slashings, who was given a very wide berth by everybody in the unit (for obvious reasons), and guess what he was given every day to take out into the garden, unsupervised... A pair of secateurs! He would get these from the officer and stick them in his overalls pocket. The drill was that if you wanted the secateurs you had to ask him for them and he would hand them to you. You then gave them back to him when you had finished and he would place them back in the pocket of his overalls. They were his secateurs. Other tools were issued each time we gardened: a garden pitchfork, a mattock and a couple of shovels, all deadly weapons in the hands of somebody like Dupas. Not one officer, ever – and I mean ever – came out to supervise what we were doing in the garden. Needless to say, I kept my eyes well and truly peeled when I was out there with Dupas as it would have been very easy for him to attack me with any of these potential weapons that the authorities gave him each day.

This is significant because anything could happen in the garden, and did. On one occasion, from my cell window I watched Camilleri make a shiv out in the garden. I watched him walking around with it in his hand and I watched him secrete it in a drain pipe. I saw him go to the drain pipe the next day and retrieve the knife, then walk around with it. It was when I saw him put it back that I told the screws about what I had seen. The whole joint was locked down and the knife was located. Dupas was regularly armed with a shiv and was not once stopped by the screws and searched.

The lack of supervision didn't apply only to Port Phillip. When I was later moved to Fulham Prison near Sale, the situation was the same. I was employed for a while in the garden gang, working outside the jail, and we went for days without seeing an officer while we were doing our job. The garden gang would walk around "no-man's-land" this was between the perimeter fence of the prison and the property fence-line beyond that. They were the blokes who would collect the drugs and bring them back in. The trick was to fill a tennis ball with drugs and toss it into this area for pick-up by the garden gang. There was a cursory search each afternoon. You could walk around for hours outside the jail with nobody watching. Yes, there is supposed to be electronic surveillance. But at Port Phillip, whenever there had been a drama that could have been solved if there had been CCTV footage of the incident, we were always told that the cameras weren't working. And the same applied at Fulham.

Worse than that was the "bush gang" at Fulham: the blokes who went out into the community and worked cleaning up playgrounds, building barbecue shelters and suchlike. The bush gang would pick up drugs left in a pre-determined location and bring them back into the jail. (That was one of the ways drugs were brought in, the other way being, as I've already said, with officers.) Where are the security officers when all this is going on? Well, they sit at the officers' station and the only time they get up is to conduct muster, break up a fight or have a smoke and a coffee. You can always tell when the screws have arrived for another day because the unit TV goes on and there it stays until lockdown at day's end. Most of the time they have a smoke and a coffee in the little officers' crib room within the unit, which is an even greater farce as far as supervision is concerned because they are all in there with the door closed.

This, by the way, was how the screws all developed the PPA or the PPG. The women officers develop the PPA – the Port Phillip arse – and the men the PPG – the Port Phillip gut. Their lack of fitness was amazing. On one occasion this lack of fitness was exposed, at the same time as providing great amusement for the majority of the jail. A bloke was in the hospital as a result of a being psychologically disturbed. He managed to get his pyjamas off and jump, as naked as the day he was born, over the razor-wire fence from the exercise yard in the hospital into no-man's-land. This area has a road around it and is completely unobstructed around the entire jail to enable emergency and maintenance vehicles access to the jail. To watch this bloke nude running around the jail perimeter with a posse of fat screws chasing him was hilarious. They took nearly an hour to run him down. Every time a screw got any where near him they were puffing and blowing so hard he would merely sprint past or right through

them. The whole jail was locked down because of this
security breach and you could hear the various units around
the jail cheering as the bloke ran past the screws yet again.
He didn't look too flash once they did finally catch hold of
him, though. He was given a thorough tidy up for his
troubles and put into the slot. So much for his mental state!

Dupas would try to strike the seeds he had so painstakingly
collected and dried in small pots. In the absence of potting
mix, which we weren't allowed, we had started a compost
heap – just a pile of clippings contained in a wooden box –
to help with the seed-raising process. But because we were
given no fertiliser or anything else to help the composting
along, it was taking a long while. Meanwhile, one day we
planted some tomato seeds and put them in a little hot house
that Dupas had built out of bits of plastic. It looked like a
humpy. The next day Dupas was screaming mad because
mice, which were rampant at Port Phillip, had got into the
hot house, scratched all the seeds up and eaten them. He
went berserk. We weren't allowed to have rat poison, for
obvious reasons; nor were we allowed to have mouse traps.
There was no way of catching these mice. This went on and
on, with our seeds being eaten by the mice on a daily basis.

Dupas was becoming more and more agitated about the
mice, until one day when Biff joined us. Don't forget this
bloke was in for murder and necrophilia, a thoroughly
unsavoury character whose IQ I have already referred to. We

were in the vegie garden and Biff and Dupas were digging over the compost heap when they located a mouse nest. In the nest were a number of baby mice, tiny, still blind. Dupas changed completely, so did Biff. What happened next shocked me so much that I couldn't watch after the first one. Dupas and Biff picked up each baby mouse by its tail and cut its head off with the secateurs. There was blood everywhere. Even though they were small mice these blokes had blood all over their hands and they were in seventh heaven over this. Even now, writing this paragraph, I am revolted by the memory of how these two men looked. They were both laughing almost maniacally, and having an absolute ball inflicting this extraordinary pain and death on these poor little animals. It was sickening to see the senseless pain inflicted on such tiny, defenceless creatures.

As I've said, Dupas was pudgy, fat, looked like he wouldn't be able to lift the skin off a rice pudding. In reality, the opposite was the case. I couldn't believe how strong his hands were, and his fingers in particular. Occasionally we were able to scavenge a small piece of wire that could be used to hold the fence up around the vegetable patch. We weren't given pliers but Dupas could twist the wire tighter and tighter and tighter, almost as tight as if he was using pliers, with no apparent effect on his fingers. It was something I couldn't do. If anybody couldn't open a jar in the unit after canteen, you would just give it to Dupas. One flick and the thing would be unscrewed. His ability to swing the mattock was another thing that I found amazing, even though he couldn't last for long because he was so overweight, smoked excessively and was generally unfit. Nevertheless, the force with which he hit the ground with the mattock was something I noticed the first time I saw him do it. He was a real contradiction. His looks well and truly belied the inner strength. He appeared to me as if his quiet demeanour was all part of this façade. The noisy ones, in my experience, don't do it; it's the quiet ones you have to keep your eye on. And he fitted that bill to perfection.

Chapter 6
The Garden of Eden

The future comes soon enough.

– ALBERT EINSTEIN

In jail you don't write anything down. Why? Because your cell is searched regularly by security staff and they read everything you have written. That wouldn't be so bad if they weren't so gossipy and didn't speak "in confidence" to other crooks. The screws well may deny that this happens but in fact it takes place with monotonous regularity. Further, if you are sitting writing anything down, some of the more dangerous crooks who have a fearsome reputation will walk in, pick up what you are writing and start reading it.

When I gave evidence against Dupas, the Dupas lawyers made a great deal about the fact that I had written nothing down. This is why. To be found out and then face the consequences was, frankly, not worth the risk. Yes, I made

notes about all sorts of things, but they were all innocuous –
recipes, books I wanted to read, new addresses from people
who had written to me – absolutely nothing that could be
even remotely connected to life in the unit. In addition to
the reasons above, I was not intending to hang on to events
that happened in jail. I just wanted to erase it all, get home,
go and work on a mate's farm and stay under the radar. That
obviously hasn't happened.

Because I kept no notes, I have no exact recollection of
dates but I do know about the specific nature of the incidents
that were to unfold, simply because of the profound impact
they had on me.

One morning Peter Dupas and I were walking up and
down in the chook pen and we were just chatting – about
what, I can't remember. The chook pen is separated from the
garden by a cyclone fence. Other units also used the garden.
There were three protection units and they were given
access to the garden at different times. It was one of the
Sirius West units that had access to the garden on this
particular morning. Sirius West is divided into two units:
one for blokes who need general protection or from whom
the rest of the jail needs protection, and the other for sex
offenders and paedophiles.

On this particular morning as we were walking up and
down I had not a care in the world apart from the fact I was
yet to serve four years of my minimum sentence, which
never cheered me. A young bloke appeared at the cyclone

fence, looking straight at us. He said nothing until Dupas and I walked towards him. As we got near the fence he said to Dupas, "Are you Peter Dupas?" We stopped. Dupas said "Yes." The young bloke, who was a Greek-looking boy, early twenties, straight darkish hair, slim build, let rip with a tirade of abuse. He claimed that he was some relative of Mersina Halvagis. He knew that Dupas had killed her and if he ever got the chance he would kill Dupas himself. This abuse was completely unexpected.

Having been a lawyer for many years and cross-examined probably thousands of people, I was good at judging when people were shocked and wrong footed. Dupas stopped dead in his tracks and was clearly flabbergasted, stuck for a word. This kid kept berating him for a good thirty seconds to a minute. I know that doesn't sound like a long time but try standing there copping abuse for that period and see how long it is. The kid then abruptly walked off. Dupas was stunned. He turned to me and said, "How does that cunt know I did it?" It was clear to me that this was an admission that he had killed Mersina Halvagis and that he couldn't work out how this kid could know.

I had gathered that Dupas was probably the only suspect for this murder, even though I had not read much about it in the paper. As a criminal defence lawyer, you are required day after day to look at police forensic photos depicting the most awful and violent crimes. You look at them in a clinical fashion, much as I imagine a surgeon would look at a patient opened up before them on the operating table. Then you close the book of photos and the matter is expunged from your mind until next time you need to refresh your memory by looking at the photos again. It's a defence mechanism you develop over many years because, if you took this work home with you, you would not see the distance. Hence, it was always my policy never to read articles in the newspaper about murders or other crimes. I didn't watch it on the news and I certainly didn't see films or watch television with anything to do with cops and robbers, violence, murder or anything else that might remind me of my job. Yet, in the case of Dupas's arrest for the murder of Nicole Patterson, it was almost impossible to avoid the media coverage, and it started up again on his subsequent conviction.

After I started working in the garden with Dupas, he invited me more regularly into his cell to speak to him, usually about the garden but sometimes about other things. It became obvious that he wanted to get some advice about all the cases that were still pending against him and he was most unhappy with the representation he had received from Legal Aid on the Nicole Patterson trial. As I've said before, it's amazing how many innocent blokes there are in jail.

Dupas kept saying that he hadn't killed Patterson. To me that was merely a defence mechanism: he had shut the murder out of his mind to the extent that he no longer thought of himself as the perpetrator of the crime. One thing belying that, though, was his body language. Whenever he talked about either Nicole Patterson, Margaret Maher or Mersina Halvagis, he would become sweaty and begin to shake. If he was sitting down on his bed he would start by sweating and shaking, then he would clasp his hands together. In the more advanced stages of his distress, he would place his clasped hands between his knees and press hard together. The last straw came when he started rocking backwards and forwards with his hands clasped, and on one occasion he even became a little teary.

I thought more than once, while he was in this state, that he was going to blurt out an admission to me. But such was his defence and denial mechanism that all of a sudden you could see the curtains come down over his eyes. He would sit back and unclasp his hands, and that was the end of the conversation. He had shut it out of his mind. Yet one thing Dupas couldn't shut out of his mind was the slow and steady progress the police were making in their investigations of the murders of both Margaret Maher and Mersina Halvagis.

I saw just how dangerous this man was one evening when we were sitting at the table having our dinner. A young bloke who had been in the unit for a few weeks walked by and Dupas started mumbling to himself, cursing him and saying he was going to "get" him. Dupas was highly agitated, with the sure signs of sweating and shaking, and I asked him what was wrong. He replied that he was going get this kid and he was going to kill him for something he had said about Dupas to somebody else in the unit which got back to him. I can't recall the particulars of the perceived slight that could have ended with a death; I just know that, at the time, I thought what an insignificant comment to die for.

Dupas was like a terrier with a rat: he kept on and on between the time of our meal and lock down, which was a couple of hours, about how he was going to get this kid in the morning. The young man's cell was next to mine on the upper tier and Dupas was immediately underneath. He virtually never came upstairs because he had a bad knee and he told me on more than one occasion that it pained him to walk up and down stairs.

On lockdown muster you do not have to stand by your cell doors, you can stand in the doorway and can actually be watching the TV as long as you are visible. That night I deliberately stood away from the door and as the screw came and counted me and started to lock the door I whispered that I needed to speak to him urgently after lockdown about a potential incident. Once you are locked down nobody can see any other cell from any part of the unit, let alone anything that goes on inside. The screws came back and quietly opened my door and asked me what the problem was. I told them what Dupas had said. The young man was moved instantly and I did not see him again.

Immediately on let-out the next morning, as I was walking toward the stairs, Dupas came hurtling out of his cell. He had something in his hand which looked like a shiv and started to fly up the stairs, totally out of character. I said,

"What are you doing, Pete?" He said, "I'm going to get that cunt." I said, "Well, I think he's gone, I've just walked past his cell and it's still locked and there's no one there." Dupas stopped and was visibly deflated at that comment. He then turned without a word and hobbled back down the stairs and into his cell. He did not even come out to the garden that day. Dupas had clearly been stewing on this all night and had worked himself up into such a frenzy that he was going to kill this kid, no matter what. That, to me, was indicative of what he was capable of and this was probably how he had killed before. He had worked himself into such a state that he was capable of anything.

At Dupas's trial for the Halvagis murder I was cross-examined up hill and down dale about the fact that the defence had tried unsuccessfully to locate any record of the young man being moved. The answer to that is simple. The jail system is so badly run, records are almost an afterthought. (A prime example of this relates to the record of lockdowns which I discuss in my previous book.)

Apart from these isolated incidents life dragged on. Dupas and Camilleri continued to hate each other and there was the odd punch on, knifing, rape, sexual assault, all those things that go to make up normal life in jail. The officers rarely get involved. On one occasion, I heard a crashing noise behind me and turned around to see two blokes punching on and they were punching each other flat out. I looked towards the screws station: one was sitting there eating his dinner, the other was standing with his arms folded. I couldn't believe my eyes. The two combatants literally punched each other to a standstill. They had been fighting so hard and for so long that they could not raise their arms one more time against each. Then the screws locked the unit down, grabbed the two protagonists and took them off to the slot. Talk about shutting the stable door after the horse has bolted! The duty of care clearly does not exist behind closed doors.

On one occasion, I remember, Dupas deliberately left the pitchfork in the garden. Camilleri had obviously seen him do it and later that afternoon, as I looked out my window into the garden, there was Camilleri with the pitchfork trying to stab another prisoner with it. Unfortunately for Camilleri this prisoner was in protection to protect the rest of the jail from him. Camilleri fights like a girl, and I mean that in the nicest possible way, so he was no match for this bloke, armed with a pitchfork or not. I am pleased to report that the other prisoner promptly disarmed Camilleri and gave him a belting. The pitchfork still did not come inside. Once again, there was no officer out there watching what was going on. Nobody had the faintest idea what had happened. The whole fight had taken place without anybody knowing and it wasn't until Camilleri came in with a bloodied face that it became apparent there had been a fight. The other bloke walked in and denied any knowledge of any fight – end of the matter.

Mention of the pitchfork reminds me of the young Greek man who featured at the start of this chapter. A week or so after the abusive incident through the chook pen fence, Dupas was standing in the vegie garden rolling a smoke. I was working in the garden with him. I looked up at him and he was staring at a window in the Sirius West cell block. He became agitated and began shaking and sweating. The sweating wasn't from exertion, either, I hasten to add. I said, "What's wrong Peter?" He said, "I know where that cunt lives." I said, "What are you talking about?" "That young bloke that abused me through the fence," he said, "I know which cell he lives in and I know when he goes for his medication. I'm going to get him." I didn't try to talk him out of it and this time I said nothing to the screws.

The next day, however, I did become concerned, because as we went out to do the gardening, Dupas took the pitchfork and put it behind a native shrub which was growing right next to the pathway along which the other unit would walk to get their medication. I saw him put it there and he said to me, "You'd better make yourself scarce. I'm going to get that bastard this morning." I went to the other end of the garden and pretended I'd forgotten something inside. I then went back into the unit and told the supervisor, not the screws, what was going to happen. For once, the staff moved quickly and the young man was not taken for medication. He was moved promptly to another jail.

The interesting thing about all this is that, there was no note of the transfer and Dupas was not even questioned by the screws. That was indicative of how scared everybody was of him, the screws included. He ruled the unit, but not by power; rather, he exuded his usual quiet, menacing intimidation. Dupas is "in" forever, so it is to the mutual benefit of the screws and Dupas that they try to make life easy for all concerned. It also makes Dupas easier to handle.

Chapter 7

The Wheels Start to Fall Off

I was sick, sick unto death, with that long agony; and when they at length unbound me, and I was permitted to sit, I felt that my senses were leaving me. The sentence, the dread sentence of death, was the last of distinct accentuation which reached my ears.

– EDGAR ALLAN POE, *THE PIT AND THE PENDULUM*

On 4 October 1997 the body of Margaret Maher was found dumped by the side of a road in Somerton, an industrial outer suburb of Melbourne. She had been stabbed repeatedly in a frenzied attack and her left breast had been cut off and jammed in her mouth. Police had a long and arduous journey ahead of them before Peter Norris Dupas was convicted of her murder on 17 August 2004. The prolonged investigation was testimony to the tenacity of the Homicide Squad.

The murder of Nicole Patterson took place on 19 April 1999 but Dupas was arrested and convicted of her murder before the Margaret Maher trial and it was for the death of Nicole Patterson that he was serving a life sentence without a minimum when I first met him. During that period, the Homicide Squad cleverly leaked to the media the fact that they were now investigating Peter Dupas for the murder of Margaret Maher. This had the desired effect: it completely destabilised Dupas to the extent that he started seeking me out and asking veiled questions about the Homicide Squad, police procedures and other such matters.

As I've said in my statement which is reproduced later in this book, Dupas is quiet, suspicious, introverted or introspective, socially inept and reticent. Even when he is discussing matters that he is really interested in, like the garden or the vegie patch, he does not talk in flowing phrases, but rather grabs that are short and separated by long breaks. I would describe his speech as disjointed – it seems to follow his thought process. Yet, even considering his usually disjointed speech, it was clear to me that the coppers had rattled him well and truly. The questions he asked me were halting, short or without any particular start or logical finishing point. But it was clear to me that he was asking about the Maher investigation and he was seeking my opinion without him specifically stating as much.

Even if you don't read the papers or watch TV or films in jail, it is impossible to escape what is going on with other prisoners and their court cases. The minute there is talk of a new investigation, the whole jail system is abuzz with it and everybody seems to "know" what's going on, even if most of this "knowledge" is wildly inaccurate and ill-informed. Certainly, everybody has an opinion. The entire system seems to thrive on speculation and innuendo, which, if repeated often enough by enough prison officers and crooks, eventually takes on all the gravity of Holy Writ. You can imagine the situation in a small unit such as Sirius East, where everybody lives in everybody else's pocket: the Dupas investigation was *big* news.

The police duly followed through on their media leak and served a Section 464 application on Dupas. Section 464 of the Victorian Crimes Act allows police to take a prisoner before a court and seek an order that they be granted more time to interview that prisoner in relation to offences other than those he is in custody for. The application really got to Dupas. He came to see me and showed me the Section 464 application. It was nothing out of the ordinary, except that it was for the murder of Margaret Maher. I told him of his rights and advised him that it was his right to decline to be interviewed and that the magistrate had to ask that question and record that answer. I reiterated to him the standard advice that I had given thousands of people over the years in my capacity as a criminal lawyer – that you are not obliged to answer any questions or make any statement but be under no misapprehension that anything you do say will be taken down and will be used in court.

As I have said, Dupas was very, very unhappy with the service (or lack thereof) that he had received from Victorian

Legal Aid during the Nicole Patterson trial, so I referred him to a private practitioner who I understand appeared for him on the Section 464 application.

I can clearly remember that it was late in the evening when Dupas returned from the 464 application hearing. He appeared at my door on the upper tier – which, as I've said, was most unusual. He was deeply distressed. He told me that he thought he would be charged not only with the Margaret Maher murder but maybe even with the Mersina Halvagis murder as well.

There comes a time in your life when you have to decide whether you're in or you are out. For me the time had come for me make my decision to try and find out more about what Dupas had been up to and I gently tried to get more details from him. The most obvious question was: What new or extra evidence did they have for the Maher murder? He said there had been some new forensic evidence, namely a glove, which as far as the Crown were concerned, linked him by DNA to the Maher murder. The glove had been found in the immediate vicinity of the body, it was a single glove, it was Dupas's glove and it had his DNA on it. I told him that if that was the case, he was in real bother.

That was when he blurted out: "I left no forensic evidence at Fawkner." That comment, as far as I was concerned, was a "voluntary admission against interest" (or potent evidence against the accused) that he had murdered Mersina Halvagis at Fawkner Cemetery. To me, the admission was clear and unequivocal. Then Dupas immediately volunteered that he had also left no DNA evidence on "the old sheila down the road". This was clearly a reference to Mrs Downes. Dupas had been living in Moonee Ponds at the time of her murder, "down the road" was Brunswick, and Brunswick was where Mrs Downes lived in the nursing home. Dupas was clearly admitting that he had murdered her too and that he had been sufficiently careful to leave no DNA linking him to the murder scene.

Time dragged on in jail and in due course Dupas was charged with the murder of Margaret Maher. Later he was served with a hand-up brief. A hand-up brief contains all the evidence that the Crown intends to rely on against an accused in their committal proceedings. Committal proceedings are a preliminary hearing where a magistrate decides whether there is sufficient evidence for a person to stand trial.

Dupas approached me with the hand-up brief and asked me to read it. I have been criticised roundly in some quarters for reading the brief and giving him my views on its contents. You must remember that I was in jail, in a small unit full of extremely dangerous people and dealing with probably the most dangerous one in that group of dangerous people. Dupas clearly considered me a friend and probably felt that what he said to me, as a former solicitor – and I stress the word *former* – would be privileged. There is no professional privilege attaching to me in these circumstances as I was no longer a lawyer, having been struck off. And further, like it or not, I was now involved to some degree and I thought that I may as well try and find out precisely where this bloke fitted in to all of these offences. Reading the brief ultimately took on far greater significance than I thought it would at the time.

When I read the brief the first thing I noticed was the similarities between the type of attack on Margaret Maher and that on Nicole Patterson – namely, a frenzied knife attack, removal of at least one breast and a slash to the thigh. At law this category of evidence is known as "similar fact evidence" and is very potent evidence indeed. I also noted, from what little I knew about Halvagis, that the same modus operandi seemed to apply to her murder, with the exception of the breast removal. It was then that Dupas confirmed to me, far more startlingly than in any of his other admissions, that not even the deceased would have seen him at Fawkner on the day of the murder. Given that Halvagis died after she was attacked from behind while kneeling over her grandmother's grave, this was another frank and surprising admission.

Dupas kept denying and denying that he had anything to do with the Margaret Maher murder. He didn't seem to be able to comprehend, or want to comprehend, the fact that the DNA evidence alone was probably sufficient to convict him. He was displaying real ostrich traits: stick your head in the sand, deny everything and hope it will go away. Like a lot of serial killers he was not going to help anyone catch him out.

I was moved to mainstream on 12 June 2003 and had nothing further to do with Dupas for some time. Meanwhile he was committed to stand trial and was later tried in the Supreme Court of Victoria for the murder of Margaret Maher, where he pleaded Not Guilty. His plea of Not Guilty was another indication of his ability to block the obvious from his mind and maintain a futile denial. He was convicted on 17 August 2004 and was again sentenced to life imprisonment without a minimum period being set.

I suppose it is in Dupas's interest to plead not guilty. He gets to leave the prison for each trial, get a new suit from the Salvos to wear, a change of diet and a change of scene. Is he getting more justice than most? You would have to say yes.

When I went into mainstream I made application to again become a prison listener. As a lawyer you spend most of your life counselling people anyway, so this was something I enjoyed. Some time between my move into mainstream and my move to Fulham in 2005, my application was accepted and I was designated one of the prison listeners for protection. A lot of the listeners refused to go into the protection units because of the types of prisoners they would have to talk to and associate with. Having been in protection, it didn't really worry me, so I was happy to be one of the designated listeners for protection. One afternoon I was called to Sirius East to talk to a prisoner. You are never told who the prisoner is until you arrive there. I walked into the unit and there was Peter Dupas.

After the conviction for the Margaret Maher murder, Dupas had been moved to Barwon for a change of scenery but he was now back at Port Phillip for some court-related matter. By this time he was already serving two life sentences without any minimum. But once again, the Homicide Squad had leaked to the media that there was great speculation that Dupas was going to be charged with the murder of Mersina Halvagis. This murder had taken place on 1 November 1997 and by now it was some time in 2004. Halvagis's parents had never given up hope that Dupas would be charged with the offence. He was extremely agitated again, talking about the media, but reaffirmed to me that nobody had seen him and that he'd left no DNA or other forensic evidence. This was the first time that he actually stated as a positive that he knew there were no eye witnesses to the crime. Only one person would know that, and that person was the killer.

I asked Dupas about Maher, as his appeal was pending. He didn't seem in the least bit upset and just said, "Ah well, it's happened." I asked him about Margaret Maher and his subsequent conviction and receipt of another life sentence without a minimum. He merely shrugged his shoulders and again said, "Oh well." This once more demonstrated to me that Dupas was, and probably still is, able to block these matters out of his mind and push on with living in his own little world within the prison system.

That was the last time I saw Peter Dupas until I climbed into the witness box in the Supreme Court of Victoria in August 2007.

Chapter 8

Mersina Halvagis: Evil Knows No Bounds

You present the awful, threatening and unanswerable question: how did you come to be as you are?

– HIS HONOUR MR JUSTICE FRANK VINCENT ON SENTENCING
DUPAS FOR THE MURDER OF NICOLE PATTERSON

Things were heating up for Dupas, particularly in relation to Margaret Maher. But also hanging over him was the ever-present question of the murder of Mersina Halvagis. It was clear that the police and the prosecuting authorities had one suspect for this murder and one suspect only. It was a matter of constant speculation in the media but the police were careful not to release all aspects of their investigation because they clearly wanted to keep back some matters that only the killer would have known.

The Halvagis murder was an old case but certainly not a cold case. In an attempt to try and flush additional evidence out of the woodwork, on 17 December 2004 the then police minister for the state of Victoria, Andre Hairmeyer, announced a reward of one million dollars payable to anybody who gave evidence that led to the conviction of the murderer of Mersina Halvagis. The offering of this reward did nothing to reveal any fresh evidence.

I hate writing about this period of my life because it takes me back into the depths of despair that was life at Port Phillip Prison. I was in jail with a murdering sex monster who wanted to tell me about his crimes and who wanted to use me as essentially free, in-house counsel. I was stuck, there was nothing I could do: damned if you do and damned if you don't.

I have already mentioned that you can't write anything down in jail, but you also can't talk confidentially to anybody from outside and more importantly you can't privately ring anybody. Therefore, the old adage "Loose lips sink ships" applies. If I had been on the phone and spoken to the coppers about this matter, the fact of that conversation would have almost certainly found its way back to Dupas and I would have been a dead duck, literally. In jail, if you lag, then the twisted morals that apply come into play: as a lagger you will most likely be killed. It never seems to occur to anybody to assess who the lagging has been done about or why. You are grouped into the most despicable and despised of categories: that of police informer. I was not prepared to place myself in that position but I was certainly caught in a dilemma because now, through no fault of my own, I had become involved to some degree with Peter Dupas. I now knew things that I didn't want to know and I had a feeling of dread that this would come back to haunt me at some stage in the future. However, I was not prepared to place my life on the line and say anything while I was still in custody.

On the day that Dupas first raised the Halvagis matter with me in his cell and told me how he had left no forensics at Fawkner, I noticed his body language change. He was sitting bolt upright. I noticed what I have detailed before: he started to sweat and shake, his hands clasped in front of him. Then, the more we discussed Halvagis, the more agitated he became. His clasped hands were placed between his knees and forced together. He then started to rock backwards and forwards. Dupas was sitting on his bed near his pillow. He was on my right. On his right was a panic button on the wall. It is a jail myth that this is also used by the police as a listening device in investigating matters but even if the cells were bugged it was of no concern to me.

While Dupas had already made oral admissions to me that he had left no DNA, what followed next surprised and shocked me just about more than anything in my life. Dupas, rocking backwards and forwards, suddenly stopped, looked at me, his eyes staring madly. He pointed at the panic button on the wall, which has a little microphone behind a stainless steel plate. He put his right forefinger to his mouth in a motion indicating that he didn't want to say anything and he didn't want me to say anything. Then he suddenly leapt off his bed, turned and faced me. He opened his arms in an expansive movement to indicate another person. He knelt down, despite his crook knees, on one knee, indicating that one person was on their knees or kneeling down or bending over. Then, without warning, he stood up and brought his two hands in to his chest, indicating himself. He then commenced flailing uncontrollably in a downward stabbing motion, clearly indicating to me that he was stabbing someone who was kneeling down. I was terrified. From what I knew, I was convinced I had just witnessed a re-enactment of a cold-blooded, frenzied murder and I didn't want to have anything to do with this. Dupas stopped, looked at me, then sat back down on his bed in a relaxed state. The blinds had come down yet again and there was nothing else to say. Conversation over.

I knew from that point on that, at some stage in the future, I would have to get involved in a prosecution of Dupas. This man, who has denied and denied every offence that he has ever committed, had now provided me with proof positive that he was the murderer. Why do I say that? The one thing that the police had been very careful not to release to the media was that Mersina had been kneeling down when she was attacked. They also hadn't released the fact that she was attacked from behind. Only one person could have known those two ingredients of the crime. And that was the killer.

I can remember almost staggering with shock back to my cell, closing my door and snibbing it for the remainder of the night because I felt sick – sick to my stomach that I had witnessed this appalling act. I must say I also felt some self pity in finding myself in circumstances where I had to interact with such people. But not just interact, actually live with them and spend every moment that my cell was unlocked having to deal with these people and frankly living in fear of what might become of me.

The pantomime in the cell had come out of the blue but it left me in no doubt as to Dupas's actions and the fact that he was the real killer. The final crunch came for me not long after the pantomime when we were in the garden together. As prison gardener you find all sorts of contraband hidden in the garden – usually drugs, often shivs and even on one occasion the precursor of an incendiary device. On this particular day I didn't find any drugs but I can remember I was facing the wall of Sirius West, which looks down over the vegie garden. Along that wall is a garden bed with some large shrubs growing in it. It is here that often you find the contraband. Most of it has been thrown out the window during searches; the screws are too stupid to have somebody outside watching what comes out of the windows while the searches are on.

I could see that some soil had been disturbed right hard up against the wall and then some mulch had been flicked over the disturbed soil. I scratched around and I located a large shiv. It would have been about ten inches long and looked like it had been made from a steel brace from a table tennis table which the prisoners in Sirius West constructed in the work area of the jail. It was long and had been sharpened along one side to a very long point. It was extremely sharp and had a little bit of towelling wrapped around the non sharpened end as a handle. I looked at this weapon. It was easily the most lethal weapon I had seen in jail. I was standing there looking at it with my back facing into the garden and to this day I don't know what made me do it but I said to Dupas, "Hey Pete, come and have a look at what I found."

I was still standing up against the wall and obscured by the bushes. Dupas walked over and I can still see the scene as clearly as if it was yesterday. I had the knife in my left hand and he came up to me on my left. I handed the weapon to him and he didn't say anything but I could read all the signs from his body language. Dupas started to shake, he became sweaty and he looked rather excited in a psychotic sort of way. He took the knife from me very gently and he held it in the palm of his open hand, almost as if he was weighing it up. He started moving the knife up and down in this weighing up motion, then, to my amazement, he started reciting, almost chanting in a trance-like state, the words "Mersina, Mersina, Mersina." I couldn't believe my ears. This man had completely lost the plot. I was in the immediate vicinity of a psychopath holding a large knife. More importantly a psychopath who was admitting that he was the one who had killed Mersina Halvagis and had used a knife to do so.

The only time in jail I was genuinely in fear for my life was this moment. I thought, by the look on Dupas's face and the manner in which he was behaving, that he was more than capable of killing me there and then. I tried to keep my act together and said to him "Pete, just give me the knife back, we'll chuck it in the bin."

We always used to throw any contraband we found in a waste bin which was emptied most days and so the contraband left the unit. I took the knife from him very quietly and gently and slowly walked to the rubbish bin. I threw the knife in and slammed the lid down, then walked away. By the time I got back to where Dupas had been standing, he was gone. He was back in the vegie patch, weeding away as if nothing had happened. The frightening thing about all of this was that he never once mentioned the knife after this and he seemed to shut the whole thing out of his mind yet again. But it was clear to me that he had made another admission that he killed Mersina Halvagis.

That night I hardly slept because I was concerned that this extremely dangerous weapon had been put in the rubbish bin. I went back first thing the next morning to make sure the bin had been emptied. It had been, and the knife was gone.

It was only later, after Dupas was convicted and I was able to speak to the police about this matter, that I learned of one of the things that had impressed them about my discussions with them regarding Dupas: I had noted precisely the same behaviour as they had when questioning him or dealing with him. That is, he would sweat, shake, even on occasions become a little teary, and you'd think he was about to blurt out an admission, hands clasped tightly between his knees pressed together, rocking backwards and forwards. But then it was almost as if a blind or a curtain came down across his entire face. He would suddenly change. He would look at you as if wondering who you were and what you were doing there, and all of a sudden the conversation was over. It was as if the preceding conversation had never taken place and he had never mentioned anything. It was lucky that I was able to take him further down the track in terms of admissions than the police had ever been able to. This was probably because of my background, my closeness to him and the fact that he may – and this is speculation – have thought that I would be subject to some sort of professional privilege, which of course I wasn't.

Chapter 9

A Bolt from the Blue: The Odyssey Begins

Be as great in act as you have been in thought.

WILLIAM SHAKESPEARE, *KING JOHN*

"Fraser! Officers' station, now!" It is five or six o'clock in the evening and I am in my room reading, as per usual. It is now mid-2005 and it's a few months since I was moved from maximum security to Fulham Correctional Centre, a medium- and minimum-security prison outside Sale in Gippsland, Victoria. I had eighteen months of my sentence left to go when the command was given.

I thought What now? No doubt another piece of petty jail politics in which I've managed to become embroiled. No matter how hard I tried to keep myself away from such situations, crooks would come and speak to me and then would talk to the officers saying that I had given them advice. This often caused problems for me, starting with my first day at Fulham when I got off the bus from Port Phillip. The operations manager got hold of me, sat me in a small ante room next to the strip-search room and gave me a talking-to about what I would and would not do while at Fulham. What I would not do, according to him, was give anybody advice. I didn't follow his instructions and constantly helped any blokes who needed assistance. Illiteracy in jail is breathtaking and you have no idea how many times a crook would come and knock on my unit door and ask me to read him a letter. Many of the illiterate prisoners were young and most were Aboriginal, and their lack of education is a sad indictment on our society. On one occasion I remember there was a letter from Legal Aid merely telling this kid that his case had been adjourned. It was a one-line letter and he couldn't read it.

The minimum-security section of Fulham, "The Cottages", is a horseshoe-shaped area with twenty-two cottages contained in a garden, four blokes per cottage, one small bedroom each, with a shared kitchen and lounge area, bathroom, toilet and laundry. A far cry from the stark conditions I had been used to for the first three years of my sentence. At least at Fulham I was able to run each day, and the job I had in the prisoners' property store was one that provided long hours and some autonomy in what you were given to do. The screw that ran the store was also smart enough to know that I wasn't going to steal anything and in return for me working in the store I was at least allowed to go for my run each morning.

My cottage was immediately over from the officers' station, where the staff sat and watched television or read the paper all day instead of supervising the prisoners.

As I approached the officers' station, the officer on duty came out to meet me in the garden area instead of waiting for me to approach the window, which is the usual procedure. All procedures in jail are designed to minimise the requirement for an officer to get up off his arse to do anything, so making the effort to walk out to me was unusual. He walked over to me and stood very close and whispered, almost inaudibly, that the Homicide Squad were on the phone and wanted to talk to me.

As a sentenced prisoner, you are not obliged to accept a visit from a police officer or talk to a police officer unless you consent and the screw indicated to me that, in view of my previous attitude to being interviewed by police about my former clients who were deceased as a result of the Melbourne Gangland wars, all I had to do was say the word and he would tell them I wasn't prepared to talk. Surprising as it may seem, the instant I heard it was the Homicide Squad on the phone, I knew precisely what they were ringing about and I said I would talk to them.

Over the years I have had extensive dealings with the Homicide Squad. They are elite coppers doing a tough job and once they get hold of a case they keep at it with a tenacity that others can only dream of emulating. A couple of the blokes in the squad are easily the best investigators I have seen. One in particular, Detective Senior Sergeant Ron Iddles, is in my view the best investigator in the Victorian police force. Homicide cases, by their very nature, are usually highly emotionally charged, so my relationship with the Homicide Squad has been hot and cold to say the least. They've lost their temper with me, I've lost my temper with them.

The usual cases I had conducted with the squad were felony murders – for instance, where someone is murdered during the course of an armed robbery. The crooks charged with these offences were real old-fashioned crooks and the cases were always bruising court-room contests where emotions ran high. But there are many other cases that are tragic and then you see a human side to the squad members.

One such case was that of a woman who was psychotic and delusional. She had murdered her own five-year-old daughter because she thought she was the devil and she had disembowelled the child with her own bare hands. When the father came home and found this awful sight, he called an ambulance. The ambulance officers had to cut the child's hair because they could not make the mother let go. That woman went to trial for murder in the Supreme Court and I think the trial lasted twenty-three minutes. The learned trial judge instructed the jury that they must retire and return a verdict of Not Guilty of murder by means of insanity. The woman was then certified as insane and sent to a secure mental facility. It was probably the most harrowing case I've ever worked on, to see this poor insignificant woman standing in the dock charged with murdering her own child. She was so distraught, as were the family. To watch the humane, caring way in which the Homicide Squad handled that case was a real eye opener for me.

I answered the phone. The caller said, "It's Senior Detective Paul Scarlett from the Homicide Squad here", and before he could say another word I said to him "What took you so long?" Apparently Scarlett was flabbergasted at this response. He said, "Do you know what I'm ringing about?" I said "My bet is you're ringing about Peter Dupas and Mersina Halvagis." He said, "How did you work that out?" I said "I just thought that's what you would be ringing about." He said "Will you talk to me?" I said "Yes." He said "When?" I said "Well, my diary is not exactly full at the moment." It was a fair indication of how serious the coppers were about finding out what I might have to say that Scarlett was at the jail first thing the next morning, ready to see me as soon as I was allowed to leave my cottage.

I later found out that Scarlett had been given the Halvagis murder investigation to go over yet again and see whether there was anything that could provide fresh evidence. As a tribute to Scarlett's detective and investigational skills, he is clearly able to think laterally.

One thing that came out that hadn't been investigated before was that I had been a gardener with Peter Dupas at Port Phillip and it had apparently been quite a talking point that the lawyer and the psychopath worked together in the vegie patch. It had no doubt appealed to some people's sense of the ridiculous. Scarlett knew that I had been with Dupas and had worked with him. He knew that I had spoken to Dupas about the Halvagis matter. In fact, apparently Scarlett was pretty dirty on me, because I had been giving Dupas advice, but what choice did I have? Dupas could have topped me at any time if I wasn't co-operative. What he didn't know was that I had talked to Dupas about this matter for one reason and one reason only: that I wanted to find out about Halvagis. And then, once I did, I wished to God I'd never known. I knew this information would come back to haunt me, I knew that it would land me well and truly in the spotlight again if I gave evidence, and that was something I could do without. I had had enough of the limelight because to that date virtually all the publicity surrounding me and my prosecution had been negative. Apparently Scarlett thought I would probably tell him to piss off when he rang me. But being the true professional that he is, he still had to ask the question and get an answer one way or the other.

At Fulham to go and talk to the coppers is a very, very dodgy prospect because you have to walk through a no-man's-land area where you are clearly visible to everybody in the cottages and one of the large units. I was apprehensive about this as I walked into the upstairs room and introduced myself to Scarlett. Being a no-bullshit sort of bloke, he cut straight to the chase and asked me what I knew about Dupas. I said, "Enough to have him convicted because he has made certain voluntary admissions against his interest to me."

Being an ex-lawyer, I was well able to judge the value of those admissions. As a copper, Scarlett also knew the value of a voluntary admission against interest. He said, "Are you prepared to make a statement?" and I said "Maybe, but not here." With that, he turned his open notebook around, pushed it across the table to me and proffered a pen. I said to him, "Not so fast. If you want me to stick my head in the noose for you, it will be a ride there for a ride back." I had eighteen months of my sentence to go and there was not a hope in hell of my giving evidence while I was in jail.

During the trial, Dupas's defence counsel, David Drake, kept demanding to know what "a ride for ride" meant. I kept saying to him, until I was blue in the face, that I did not say that, I said it was "a ride there for a ride back" – a colloquialism for "if you want me to do something for you, you do something for me first". In other words, you scratch my back, I'll scratch yours.

I told Scarlett that I would not make a statement there and then and would not give him any particulars, save to say that I had substantial evidence against Dupas. And I said that, by the way, I was still having difficulty with whether I wanted to give evidence. I knew giving evidence was the right thing to do morally but I really didn't want to put myself or my family in any danger and I did not want a lot of unpleasant publicity and attendant media, which it was as sure as eggs I would attract.

The clincher for me was when Scarlett said to me, "You have a daughter, don't you?" The answer to that was Yes. She was a young girl at that time and I sat and thought for a moment. I thought about the Halvagis family whose story it had been impossible to miss in the media, and I decided there and then to give evidence.

I told Scarlett that I was a man of my word and now that I had committed to it, I would do so. However, there were pre-conditions. He said "What about the reward?" As I said earlier, as a matter of policy I don't read newspaper stories about cops and robbers and it follows that I don't read about rewards. I said to him "I assume there is a reward." He said "Do you know how much it is?" I said "No, but once again I'll have a guess and say its a hundred thousand, which is the usual reward posted for a murder." He said "Well, try a million dollars." I nearly fell off my chair. That was not, and I repeat not, the motivation for my giving evidence. The fact that I too had a daughter *was*. I then pointed out to Scarlett that his having come to the jail and my talking to him was highly dangerous and that I would under no circumstances make a formal statement or give evidence while I was in custody. I wanted to be released a year early. Scarlett indicated that he would take that back to his superiors but his preliminary view was that he wouldn't have a problem with that proposition.

I gave Scarlett a very scant oral outline and he left our first meeting at Fulham with a few notes and nothing more. I was now highly excited yet apprehensive at the prospect of an early release. But I was most concerned about the involvement I would have to have with the police in giving evidence at a trial and about all the attendant dangers. The reward was not a major part of my thinking. Obviously the prospect of a large sum of money, when I had lost everything, was attractive but as I write this book, I have been home for more than two years, my parole has expired and I have not received one cent from anybody as a result of giving evidence because Dupas, after his conviction, appealed.

I contacted my lawyer immediately and received a visit during which we discussed the matter and particularly the prospect of my going home early. Later I discussed with my then wife the prospect of coming home early but having to stick my neck out. The general consensus was that it was something I should do and they would support me. I contacted Scarlett and he came and saw me again and I told him I was prepared to make a "Can Say Statement", which means that the contents of the document are indicative of the sworn evidence I could give if I were called upon to do so but it is not a formal statement. The only basis on which I participated at all in the Can Say Statement was that the Petition of Mercy to get me out early could not be considered until there was evidence before the Director of Public Prosecutions that would indicate that granting that Petition of Mercy would be beneficial to the trial.

A third visit to Fulham was organised for me to finalise my Can Say Statement. I told the police that having coppers wandering in and out of the jail to see me was far too dangerous. I didn't care what pretence they used; news spreads like wildfire in the jail environment and I was trying to avoid having any awkward questions asked of me. The screws talk and loose lips can land you in all sorts of bother.

To cover my tracks, the Homicide Squad issued an application pursuant to Section 464 of the Crimes Act, which, as I've mentioned before, allows them to remove a prisoner from jail to make an application to a court for the prisoner to be questioned further. This application was made to a magistrate at Sale and was made suggesting I had been involved in a fraud. Only the magistrate and the Homicide Squad knew that the 464 was merely a ploy to get me out of jail. I was taken to the court and then directly to the Sale Police Station, where the Homicide Squad were waiting for me. I then spent some time making my Can Say Statement.

Once the statement was finished and I had signed it, a copy went to David Grace QC, my lawyer, and he made an application for a Petition of Mercy to the Attorney General but it had to be the Attorney General in Canberra because I was charged with a Commonwealth offence. For the Petition of Mercy to have any hope of success the Victorian Director of Public Prosecutions, Paul Coghlan QC, also had to support the petition being granted. The Can Say Statement was finalised on 28 June 2005.

I asked to be released in November 2005, one year early. Nothing happened. It then turned out that the coroner had been given a brief of evidence for the Halvagis murder a year before and had gone no further because there was insufficient evidence to potentially support a finding of guilt against Dupas. All the witnesses who ultimately gave evidence had come forward by then and it was considered that the brief of evidence wasn't strong enough to secure a conviction. November 2005 came and went. I wasn't getting out a year early. Then the Homicide Squad told me that I would probably be out in February 2006, as that was when the inquest was starting into Halvagis, and Dupas was the only suspect.

The inquest began in February amid a media frenzy and Coghlan himself was prosecuting. He made the unusual statement in open court that he was sure that Dupas was the killer but there was insufficient evidence for him to be charged. The inquest came and went. I was still not released. I was really starting to wonder whether all of this was a wind-up. Each time the Homicide Squad spoke to me they said I would be released yet I wasn't. I'm not blaming them but I'm most unhappy with my treatment by the Director of Public Prosecutions.

Matters became so protracted that the Attorney General's office in Canberra rang Coghlan wanting to know what was going on with the DPP's support because they were ready to grant the petition. All that was required was a letter from Coghlan. I'd love to know why it was delayed for a year when it was clear that nothing was happening until such time as I was out and about.

I spoke to David Grace regularly and it got to the stage where, with a couple of months to go, he told me that I might as well get my head around doing the lot and that there would be no discount. The question for me then was whether I would still be prepared to give evidence. The Homicide Squad were justifiably anxious that I might change my mind if I got no reduction in the sentence. I was still prepared to give evidence and told the police so on a number of occasions.

You cannot receive calls in jail unless they are from lawyers or the police. Late in the evening on Thursday 5 September 2007, David Grace called the jail and asked to speak to me. The screws couldn't find me, so Grace left a message that I should ring his office urgently, which I subsequently did. He said "You are going home on Monday, a mere two months early but better than no early release at all." I hung the phone up and cried, the wait and speculation was over.

I was to be released on 9 September 2006, a mere two months before my due release date of 11 November 2006. Coghlan had sat on my application for twelve months. This whole thing had been held up inexplicably for over a year by the DPP's reluctance to say that I should be released early. The Homicide Squad were among the losers: they knew full well that I would not give evidence until I was released. And they could not charge Dupas until I was released.

What followed was a complete and utter bun fight. My release was supposed to be, as arranged with the Homicide Squad, what is known as a "controlled extraction". This means nobody was to know that I was going. My parole papers were to be faxed through to the jail to the intelligence section. That was run by Ms Kaye and she is about the only person at Fulham who seems to know which way is up. I was supposed to be taken from my work in the property store to my cell, pack up and be put out the door without talking to anybody or anyone being any the wiser until I was gone. This was all designed to minimise any chance of harm befalling me on the way out.

Instead, on the Friday about lunchtime, I was called to the Shift Office, which is right in the hub of the jail, next to the canteen, the library and the medical centre. At this time on a Friday there are hundreds of prisoners milling around the area waiting for their weekly canteen visit. As I walked down to the Shift Office a couple of prisoners said to me, "You're going home on Monday. Good on ya, well done. What's happened?" Blah blah blah. I was horrified.

I walked into the Shift Office and rather than seeing Kaye for a controlled extraction, a prison officer started reading out all the stuff about what I'd had to say and that I'd been granted a Petition of Mercy by the Commonwealth and I was to be released early on twenty-six months' parole. I told him that this was highly sensitive and he shouldn't be reading it out in front of all these other officers and crooks. He said "Bad luck. That is the way it's being done." I then had to sign the form and wandered off. For the remainder of Friday, all of Saturday and until late on Sunday, I was left in the mainstream prison population. If, during that time, the slightest whisper had got out that I was giving Crown evidence, I would have been dead.

The operations manager, Andy Walker (aka The Barrel), then came and saw me on Sunday and said that he was going to slot me until Monday morning as I was in danger. In the entirety of my sentence, I hadn't been in solitary and I jacked up and refused to go. He said "If you don't go, I'll drag you." I still flatly refused. By this stage, there was a constant stream of blokes in and out of my cottage enquiring as to how come I was going home early. The story I put about was that I had got two months off because of the length of my sentence and a Petition of Mercy had been successful.

I demanded to know why I had been left in the prison population since Friday lunchtime when it became general knowledge that I was going home and why there hadn't been a controlled extraction. Amazingly, in relation to my going home early, he said "I didn't know." I was flabbergasted. I had nothing to lose now. I leant across the desk and I said to him, "That is a bloody joke. You are supposed to know."

With that he said, "I'll do a deal. I'll put you in the hospital rather than the slot. The hospital is next to the slot. And you will be released at 5 am to avoid a media scrum because let-out time is usually 7 am."

I was unceremoniously escorted to the hospital where I was placed in a single room, which may as well have been a solitary cell. I was finally given a small television to watch. I asked for dinner. Dinner time came and went. I am still waiting. I then asked for a cup of tea. I am still waiting. At five o'clock the next morning, after a sleepless night, the screws came and got me and took me to the discharge. I was unceremoniously shoved out the door with the words "Fuck off" ringing in my ears.

Four years and ten months were now over and I was a free man. The party was about to start.

Chapter 10
Hot on the Trail

Never write anything down unless you are prepared to
have it read out in court.

– OSCAR WILDE

The purpose of a statement is to set out formally and under
oath the evidence you would be able to give if called upon
at trial. This document forms the basis of your evidence
and that is what's referred to in the law as evidence in
chief. When and if you are called at trial, that is the initial
sworn evidence you give in response to prosecutors'
questions.

You may then be cross-examined by the defendant's
lawyer as to any inconsistencies, omissions or lies that the
defence allege arise from the statement. My statement was
compiled over three sessions with Paul Scarlett and I
reproduce the statement in this chapter to give you a flavour

of just where my thoughts were and how a statement is made and comes to be given in evidence. The statement is scanned straight into this chapter so you can read it in its entirety.

In paragraph 19 I refer to Kathleen Downes's murder and in paragraph 20 I refer to my discussions with Dupas about similar fact evidence against him in the Halvagis case which arose from his murders of Maher and Patterson. The police said both of these comments should not be in the statement as their prejudicial value outweighted their probative value. That particular objection is commonly made in the legal process and it results in a statement being edited before it goes to the jury. I objected to having those phrases deleted because they were an integral part of my statement and if they were to be deleted then that could be done after a defence application.

The trial began and as expected defence counsel made application for those paragraphs to be deleted. That application was successful and those two pieces of evidence did not go before the jury. On this occasion those two paragraphs were removed from the statement that went to the jury. In other words, the jury never knew about that evidence.

You will note my statement is made up of three separate discussions as I have stated above. I wished the statement to properly reflect each conversation that had taken place with the police so there could be no suggestion of invention on my part. Of course, the standard allegation of fantasy was thrown at me when I gave evidence on Dupas's trial.

When I stepped into the witness box, my statement, complete with the passages later deleted, was tendered as my evidence in chief by the Prosecutor, Colin Hillman QC.

Andrew FRASER

STATES :

1.　　　My name is Andrew Roderick FRASER, date of birth 5 April 1951. I am currently a prisoner at Fulham Correctional Centre, Sale serving a term of imprisonment for being knowingly concerned with the importation of a commercial quantity of cocaine and trafficking cocaine.

2.　　　I was imprisoned on 13 November 2001 and was moved to Port Phillip Prison ("PPP") in February *(date to be confirmed)* 2002. I was placed against my wishes into the protection unit, Sirius East at PPP. There I remained until being finally moved to mainstream at PPP on 12 June 2003 and thereafter on 6 January 2005, I was moved to Fulham Correctional Centre.

3.　　　While at Sirius East, I met Peter Norris DUPAS and became close to him. We were the two gardeners for the protection units and spent a large proportion of each day together working in the garden. We also undertook education together studying horticulture and used to watch gardening and associated programmes together on TV.

4.　　　I have been approached by Detective Senior Constable Paul SCARLETT of the Homicide Squad who enquired as to whether as a result of my association with DUPAS I knew anything of the murder of Mersina HALVAGIS and further whether I would be prepared to give evidence against DUPAS. I am able to say that DUPAS discussed HALVAGIS with me and made certain admissions, voluntarily and against his interests and subject to certain preconditions being met, I am prepared to execute a formal statement and give evidence if required.

5.   By way of background, I say that in jail the etiquette is that you never ask another prisoner what they are "in" for, or the circumstances surrounding their incarceration; to be nosey is to invite violence and I have witnessed such attacks.

6.   As a result of the foregoing, I did not ask DUPAS any questions and was early in the piece concerned not to upset him, or appear overly inquisitive as I consider him to be probably the most dangerous person I have met and I did not want to be attacked. It was only over a period of time DUPAS and I started to talk and it was only after the MAHER investigation got into top gear that he was clearly rattled and opened up to me more.

7.   At this point, I should say a little about DUPAS, he is very quiet, suspicious, introverted or introspective, socially inept and reticent to talk. Even when discussing matters of interest, he tends not to speak in flowing phrases, rather grabs of sentences, short, followed by long breaks. I did observe when agitated or anxious he would start to shake and on occasions became teary and often when that happened, he would clam up and the conversation would be over. He was very difficult to communicate with but over the period from when I went to PPP and DUPAS was moved to Barwon, approximately 1-2 months before I went to mainstream, he opened up to me as much as I think he is capable of.

8.   I also think based on years of dealing with these types of offenders, that he has blocked a lot of his offending out of his mind and when the memory returns, this is when he becomes distressed.

9.   The first indication of DUPAS' involvement with the HALVAGIS murder came before the MAHER investigation. At Port Phillip the protection unit is divided into three, Sirius East and West. West is divided into two, A & B side. This is done because of the different types of protection required. East's for the worst of the worst, that it is considered everyone wants to get. This is where I was placed.

10.   West's roughly divided into sexual offenders on one side and those too violent or unreliable to be in the general population. The garden area therefore has different access times for the three units. At the back of Sirius East is a small "chook pen" exercise yard and this looks onto the garden and the other units can see into this yard when they are in the garden. It is separated only by a mesh fence.

11.   DUPAS and I were alone walking in the chook pen when one of the other units had use of the garden. It was early in the morning and before the MAHER investigation caused DUPAS to be interviewed. He had not mentioned HALVAGIS to me at all. A younger Greek looking prisoner, I don't know his name, came right up to the fence and said are you Peter DUPAS: Yes. He then commenced to berate DUPAS saying HALVAGIS was a cousin of his. DUPAS was an animal; he knew DUPAS had killed Mersina and that if he got a chance he would kill DUPAS.

12.   This verbal attack was out of the blue and DUPAS was clearly shaken by the barrage. He turned to me shaking and said, his exact words were "How does that cunt know I did it?" I was surprised at his admission because he was saying he had done it. I remember this because it was significant.

13.   About a week later we were in the veggie garden when I noticed DUPAS looking at one of the upper windows of Sirius West, he was starting to shake, a sure sign to me he was agitated. I asked what he was looking at and he told me he now knew which cell the abusive one was in and he was going to try and "knock" him because he would not be allowed to go around saying such things. I took this utterance seriously.

14.   A short number of days later we were again in the garden when DUPAS said that he knew when that person would be going to see the doctor and he was going to jump him then and kill him. He told me in no uncertain terms not to be in his way and it would be better if I was elsewhere as he did not want me involved. He took the garden fork and put it where it could not be seen near the pathway. Luckily that person did not go to the doctor that day and was shortly thereafter moved. Nothing further came of that incident.

15.   When the police let the media know that DUPAS was again being investigated for the MAHER murder DUPAS' demeanour changed markedly, it was at this time he started to ask me questions. It was never a discussion, always short questions or series of questions that seemed to have no starting or finishing point but to me it was clear that he was asking me about MAHER and seeking my opinion.

16.   As s.464 application was served and he was obviously and deeply distressed, he asked me about the procedure and I told him he could decline to consent and he did not have to answer questions. I referred him to a private practitioner for advice as he was dissatisfied with Legal Aid.

17.   At this stage I am unsure of the exact chronology, but with further thought and checking of dates I will be sure. You must remember this approach came out of the blue and I had not prepared a draft prior to this.

18.   When DUPAS was interviewed pursuant to s.464 he came back to jail and he immediately sought me out in my cell, he was upset and said he thought he would not only be charged with MAHER but maybe HALVAGIS. I thought it was time to try and gently coax the story from him. I asked what the new or extra evidence they had for MAHER. DUPAS said there was mention of forensic evidence, a glove. He then made a surprising admission to me that, "He left no forensic evidence at Fawkner". This clearly meant HALVAGIS.

**REMOVED BY
ORDER OF THE
TRIAL JUDGE**

21.　　　I emphasised the potential problem with the glove containing DNA traces at the MAHER scene and he again stressed he left no DNA or forensics at the HALVAGIS scene.

22.　　　I cannot recall at what stage of proceedings he was moved to Barwon but he was subsequently convicted and sentenced in the MAHER matter.

23.　　　About mid to late 2004, I became a prison listener at PPP. This is a peer support job and prisoners discuss their problems with you. I was in mainstream by this time but was one of the designated listeners for protection. I was called to see a prisoner at Sirius East and I was surprised to see it was DUPAS, he was back at PPP for some court reason which I do not recall.

24.　　　　There had been more publicity and media speculation regarding HALVAGIS and again he was upset. The crux of this conversation was again that he could not be charged because lack of evidence, i.e. no forensics left at the scene by him and no-one could have witnessed the attack because no-one was around. This is the first time he actually stated as a positive that he knew there were no witnesses, it was clear to me that there was only one way he would have known that fact and that is, he is the killer.

25.　　　　He did not seem the least bit perturbed by this conviction regarding MAHER, he said effectively "Oh well".

26.　　　　I did not have any further discussion with DUPAS after that. PPP would have a record on the running sheets of when I went to see DUPAS for the last time.

27.　　　　I am prepared to give this evidence and make a formal statement as required.

28.　　　　Some of these incidents may be out of order. I would need to access dates etc. to be more specific.

FURTHER COMMENTS TO DRAFT STATEMENT

OF ANDREW RODERICK FRASER

To Paul SCARLETT

Dear Mr SCARLETT,

29)   When you first arrived and spoke to me unannounced, I was caught somewhat by surprise regarding the matters raised and accordingly the previous "can say" statement I provided was missing some important details. You must appreciate that it is only since your representations that I have given this matter detailed thought.

30)   Hereunder are now further aspects of this case that have come to mind since my previous statement. If further detail comes to me I will advise.

31)   I have now spoken to Michael BRERETON and David GRACE who agree with the suggested course as does my wife Denise even though I will no doubt receive further publicity which, while it should be positive for me, I can do without it.

The additional matters are:-

32)   In the discussion I had with DUPAS in his cell about HALVAGIS and him not leaving any forensics at the scene, I add that his body language is easy to read, he sits upright when anxious or stressed, stares ahead, starts to shake (and can even be a bit teary) and he folds his hands and clamps them between his knees. He rocks back and forth a little bit but it is noticeable.

33)   This is how DUPAS was sitting when talking about HALVAGIS but then he jumped up and did a little pantomime of a person leaning over which I took to be HALVAGIS followed by his demonstrating a stabbing motion on the other person. He lifted his hand up about shoulder high and executed a swift, sharp downward motion. He did not speak while he did this but the meaning was obvious and not at all ambiguous, he was demonstrating his killing of HALVAGIS.

34)   He then sat back on his bed, hands between his knees and the conversation was over.

35)   I should say here that all his admissions are short and not detailed. DUPAS is very introverted and I would say almost sociopathic, he does not relate well to others and has great difficulty talking to others. His conversations with me were always short and sometimes finished abruptly as above described.

36)   The first occasions DUPAS made any mention of any killing was well before he was charged with the MAHER matter. Ray EDMUNDS, Paul GORMAN, DUPAS and I were in the workshop doing "nuts and bolts", i.e., putting sleeves and nuts on locks in bolts. No-one else was there and we went there occasionally to have a quiet chat. It was on this day *(I don't know the date)* that I was talking to EDMUNDS re his sentence. At that stage, he had served about twenty years and I asked how he handled it. His response was he had done what he had done, a bad offence, regretted it and had paid and was continuing to pay a heavy price. GORMAN then admitted his offences (rape) and said he was near the end of his sentence and upon release he would probably re-offend as he could not help himself. DUPAS was next to EDMUNDS and EDMUNDS said, "What about you Pete?" DUPAS hesitated and all was quiet, he then haltingly admitted the killing of Nicole PATTERSON.

37)   I was surprised because he pleaded not guilty. He was not remorseful, rather off-hand in fact, "What's done is done and I have to wear it". I then admitted my offence as I did not want to be the odd man out.

38)   Finally as evidence of propensity to violence and in addition to the comments about the planned attack on another prisoner in the garden I previously mentioned, there was another incident between DUPAS and another prisoner. DUPAS is quite spooky, very quiet and you have no idea what he is thinking. We were sitting at a table having dinner and he indicated another prisoner who he perceived had slighted him in some way. DUPAS was mumbling about getting him. I thought nothing more of it until before lockdown when he kept saying he was going to get him in the morning. To "get" in jail means to attack with a view to inflicting serious harm or death. DUPAS mentioned this a few more times that evening. He was shaking and I took this threat so seriously I mentioned it to the officers. On lock up DUPAS told me he was going to get him first thing next morning because the staff are usually outside having a coffee and a smoke and the unit is quiet.

39)   On let out DUPAS came flying up the stairs, this was unusual because he has a bad knee and avoids the stairs, even to come to my cell. I saw he had an implement which looked sharp in his hand, he said "where is he" and I told him the person in question had been moved last night. He appeared deflated and went back downstairs. My opinion is he had stewed on this all night and had worked himself into a state by the next morning. He was ready for and capable of anything in my opinion.

Yours faithfully,

AR FRASER

40)   My full name is Andrew Roderick FRASER and my date of birth is the 5th of the 4th, 1951. I have attended at the Sale Police Station today at the request of Detective Sénior Constable SCARLETT. I have been shown the above document and I agree that this is a copy of two draft statements that I had previously prepared for SCARLETT. As I read through this document on the computer I made a couple of changes mainly grammatical ones.

41)   In relation to paragraph 11, SCARLETT has asked for further information as to who this person was that abused DUPAS and when in time this event took place. All I can suggest is that it was probably 6 months after I started gardening with DUPAS. I had probably been at Port Phillip Prison for about 8 months at this stage. I can't recall any details as to who this person was as I met so many people in jail and I never took any notice as to who they all were. I can say he looked to be young, by that I mean early 20's and approximately 5 foot 7 inches tall, light build, olive complexion, brown eyes, straight black hair with a longish fringe that he kept flicking back. It was clear to me that he was Greek.

42)   In relation to paragraph 13, I would like to add that at the time I noticed DUPAS shaking, it was obvious to me because at the time he was trying to roll a cigarette and was having trouble doing so. DUPAS is a heavy smoker and usually had no difficulty rolling his cigarettes. I have also used the word "knock", that is jail term for killing.

43)   In relation to paragraph 17, I would like to add that this approach came out of the blue and was made to me by the Homicide Squad. I did not approach the prosecution. For this reason there is more than one draft statement as particulars came back to me over a period of time. I had not prepared a draft statement prior to this.

44)   In relation to paragraph 20 I want to mention that paragraph 33 also relates to this same conversation with DUPAS. I want to add that at the time of having this conversation with DUPAS and him stating there were no witnesses, he was sitting on his bed in his cell near the head of the bed. I was sitting on the bed at the foot. On the wall at the head of the bed is a loud speaker / panic button which is screwed into the wall, it is generally accepted by prisoners that this piece of equipment is used as a listening device by staff and often prisoners refuse to talk in their cells for this reason.

45)   I had read the brief and indicated to him the matters raised in paragraph 20. I wish to add that in addition to the verbal admission made that he left no forensics at the scene of the HALVAGIS murder, he was adamant there were no eye witnesses. He pointed at the speaker on the wall as if to say "no more talk" and with that jumped to his feet, turned and faced the bed and used a downward opening motion of his arms and indicated a person bending forward. He stood back and with an arm movement then indicated himself and further he indicated a raised right arm and then a downward stabbing motion. This indicated to me how he had killed HALVAGIS and why she would not have seen him.

46)   I have been requested by SCARLETT to remove paragraph 19 from this previously drafted statement as it relates to a matter not relevant to SCARLETT's investigation. I have requested that it remains in until directed by the Office of Public Prosecutions.

47)   Further to the above two statements, thereafter on the 24th of June, 2005, I provided a further draft can say statement. It reads as follows:

Further statement of Andrew FRASER; further to previous draft statements made by me I wish to add the following which has come to mind after giving this matter further considerable thought.

LUNATIC SOUP

48)   It has been annoying me that I have not been able to adequately describe the way DUPAS communicates. I have previously described it as speaking in grabs or snatches, the word I have been searching for is "disjointed", in other words his conversations do no flow. In addition he appears to keep himself under a tight rein and occasionally things get the better of him and he will utter something that he almost instantaneously regrets and he clams up again.

49)   You can almost watch the pressure build, he becomes obviously anxious, commences to shake and little sweat around his temples. He then utters what ever it is he says and almost immediately you can see him check himself and the conversation is over.

50)   I have had many years dealing with criminals and I have dealt with many murder trials. It is my opinion based on that experience that DUPAS is probably the most dangerous and unpredictable person I have ever met.

51)   I have now recalled when on my run on Wednesday the 22nd of June, 2005, that in the garden at PPP DUPAS and I regularly found contraband hidden in the garden; drugs, knives and on one occasion part of what I would describe as an incendiary device. DUPAS always threw these items into the rubbish bin and instructed me to do likewise, otherwise the bringing of these items to the attention of Officers usually resulted in a lock down and search and you could be locked down for days as has happened on more than one occasion following items being located in the jail.

52)   On one day I recall clearly I was weeding a garden bed outside Serious West Unit and uncovered a substantial home made knife. The knife appeared to me to be made from a table tennis brace and was very professional. One side had been ground down (usually done on one of the concrete pathways) and had a taped handle. I called DUPAS over and showed him the item as was usual when we found something. He looked at the knife, he was on my left, and took it from me. He started to move the knife up and down as if feeling the balance of the item. He started to sweat and looked me with a very strange look on his face, I was apprehensive at this time and he uttered one word "Mersina" (I am unsure of the spelling) and handed the knife back. I put it in the bin but was shaken by the incident. I had no doubt that he was referring to the deceased HALVAGIS and had no doubt he was telling me he had stabbed and killed her with a similar instrument.

53)   I was so concerned by this that the next day I checked the bin had been emptied and that the knife was gone.

54)   My memory of this was prompted when I saw a couple of prisoners obviously secreting something in long grass last Wednesday as above mentioned.

55)   This should be part of my statement.

Statement taken and signature witnessed by me
At Sale Police on 28/06/05 at 12.35 pm.

P. SCARLETT
D/S/C 28414

LUNATIC SOUP

I hereby acknowledge that this statement is true and correct and I make it in the belief that a person making a false statement in the circumstances is liable to the penalties of perjury.

Andrew FRASER

Acknowledgment made and signature witnesses by me
At Sale Police Station on 28/06/05 at 12.36 pm.

P. SCARLETT
D/S/C 28414

Chapter 11

Take a Deep Breath: The Preliminary Hearing

Once more unto the breach dear friends, once more.

– WILLIAM SHAKESPEARE, *HENRY V*

September 11 2007 was my release date. The irony of the date certainly has not been lost on me.

Every day of your sentence you calculate how long you have done and how long you have got until you go home. Everybody, even the homeless, refers to getting out as "going home". Going home dominates your thinking and you wonder day in and day out what it will be like when your turn comes because, with a few exceptions, everybody's turn comes, no matter how long the sentence.

Year after crushing year, the time drags interminably. The only thing that keeps you going is the thought of what will happen on the day you go home. Judges, when they sentence you, recite a po-faced mantra about not imposing crushing sentences, about rehabilitation, about family, job prospects when you get out … on and on they rabbit.

All these pronouncements count for nothing. Sentencing is nothing more these days than a box-ticking exercise enabling a judge to cover his own behind in case of appeal by either defence or the DPP. There is nothing intuitive about sentencing these days because if a judge gives somebody a bit of a go, it is often the case that the Director of Public Prosecutions will then appeal against the leniency of the sentence and in the current political climate such appeal is often successful with the sentence being increased.

When I say it is a box-ticking exercise I mean it literally. All the criteria for sentencing are enumerated in a handbook. The judge's handbook is needed because gone are the days when every judge is appointed with sufficient experience and knowledge in a given field for them to run a court by experience. These days there are judges and more particularly magistrates who are appointed and have never conducted a case in court off their own bat. The judge's little helper (the handbook) sets out the various aspects of sentencing that must be addressed when a judge passes sentence and as long as he/she has ticked all the boxes, then on appeal by the accused, providing the judge has covered himself adequately the appeal will fail, it won't matter whether the penalty is unnecessarily heavy; the Court of Appeal wheels out its favourite old chestnut that the sentence is "not manifestly excessive". See you later!

Not only are some judges and magistrates inexperienced in court when appointed (which one would have thought essential for being appointed), the real problem is a judicial officer's inability to empathise with the man in the street. A quick scan of the background of most appointments is private school, university and the legal profession. Such are the pressures stupidly imposed by the tertiary establishments that students have no, or very little, life experience outside this cosseted existence. How, then, can they even begin to understand how circumstances dictate the common people's actions?

I wonder if sentencing would be the same if all judges were required to serve only one day's imprisonment. Not five years, just one day. My bet is that the reality check in that one day would be sufficient for judges to be far more humane in their sentencing. In my view the court system has lost touch with not only the very community they are supposed to administer but with reality itself. You only need to read some judgements to grasp this argument very quickly. The law truly has become an ass!

Every day of the week in the popular media you hear people screaming about sentences being inadequate. The reality is that sentences have increased exponentially, particularly in relation to drug and violence offences. I can remember when I was a junior solicitor handling a culpable driving trial in Bendigo. The late, great Brian Nettlefold QC appeared for the accused. We went to a trial, the accused pleaded Not Guilty and was convicted. Because the young man was a university student from a good home and highly unlikely to transgress again, he was given a suspended sentence. These days such a penalty would be unheard-of and immediately appealed by the DPP if it were imposed.

The young man concerned had been driving home from university for the weekend with a mate in the car. They were drinking while driving. He was on the wrong side of the road passing another car when a motor cyclist came over the brow of the hill in the opposite direction and there was a head-on collision. The motorcyclist's face was embedded in the roof of the car just above the windscreen – you could see the deceased's face print. The reason the young man didn't see the motorcyclist in time was because he had his head tilted back drinking beer from a can. The speedo jammed on impact at 80 miles per hour – approximately 140 kilometres per hour. Both of the young men in the car walked away with relatively minor injuries. The motorcyclist was killed on impact. These days he would be a certainty to receive a sentence somewhere in the vicinity of six or seven years; if he did well, maybe three or four.

That is merely an example of what sentencing was like in the good old days, by contrast with now. The other penalty that has increased out of sight, but far more quickly, is that for murder. If you have a look at murder sentences fifteen years ago, the average domestic murder received a sentence of somewhere in the vicinity of ten to twelve years. These days, twenty years is common. Who says sentences haven't increased? Who says sentences are inadequate? And these days judges hand them out willy-nilly – and frankly, in my view, with little regard for the wreckage they cause.

And so it is that you wait for the day. You wait and wait. Finally it has arrived. What's it going to be like? Believe it or not, even though I battled against institutionalisation, I still think that I probably was to some degree institutionalised as a result of the period of time I spent inside and the circumstances in which I spent it.

I was marched out the door unceremoniously, sent on my way with a typical farewell from one of the screws. It was over. I stood with my back to the fence, a little like a rabbit caught in the head lights, and wondered what awaited me. I knew I had let myself in for plenty of publicity and I was ready for whatever came my way in that respect; I just wasn't expecting it quite as soon as it hit.

I jumped into a friend's car and we headed off towards Melbourne. Fulham is a good couple of hours from the city and not much was open at that hour of the morning. We found a McDonald's and had a coffee. Compared to the jail coffee, this tasted like nectar. We had to wait until nine o'clock for the shops to open so I could get some clothes. I refused to wear one item that I had worn in jail. Apart from what I was wearing, I gave everything away to crooks still inside who were worse off than I was.

We drove to Chadstone Shopping Centre and arrived in time for David Jones to open. There I purchased new socks and jocks, bolted into the changing room, changed, threw the last vestiges of my jail attire in the bin and was away. I already felt like a new person.

Because I was out early and unexpectedly, I had nothing planned for the day or the week ahead. My marriage had failed, so I had to set up a completely new home from scratch. Off we trotted to the supermarket, where I used borrowed money to buy all the basics – enough to get me going. I was going to live in a house offered by a friend in Canterbury Road, St Kilda, back in my old stomping ground. So we drove to Acland Street where we had another coffee – a real one this time. Fantastic. Back in the real world. I must say, I received a lot of assistance from friends on that first day out, and I will be eternally grateful for that assistance.

Although I was enjoying myself I still felt extremely strange. Even now, after two years, I can't adequately describe the feeling I had that day. It was sort of a numbness but at the same time quite a buzz. It certainly was not the euphoria I had anticipated when I had endlessly imagined this day. I have read Peter Carey's book *Bliss*, where the main character almost dies and suffers an out-of-body experience. This is exactly what the first day was like, I can see me standing away from myself and observing, it was quite a weird feeling watching what was taking place.

I didn't have a job or an income, so my next priority was to visit the dole office. While I was in jail at Fulham, there was one officer whose title was the oxymoronic "prisoner welfare officer". About two weeks before I was released I went to see this officer and told him that I was likely to be released shortly, maybe even early. I filled out all the forms and when I was released all I had to do was present at the dole office with a slip of paper which he gave me and all would be fixed: the unemployment benefit would be waiting, as would be the Medicare card.

Having checked out my new home and dropped off the groceries, I was at the Centrelink office in South Melbourne by ten o'clock. I walked in with my receipt and the bloke who served me looked at the piece of paper and said "What's this?" I explained to him what I had been told. He checked his computer and he said, "Well, I can tell you nothing's been done, nothing's been lodged and there is no unemployment benefit for you." Two hours later, I left with an emergency payment of a few dollars and no Medicare card. Thank you very much to Fulham Correctional Centre for properly looking after my "welfare". I know it's popular to bag Centrelink but I should give a tick where it is deserved: all the people I had dealings with at Centrelink were patient and caring, and nothing was too much trouble. They helped me through a difficult period and I thank each and every one I dealt with.

I strolled out of the dole office into the beautiful spring day and as I had no car I decided to walk from South Melbourne to the Albert Park Deli and have another coffee (guess what I missed most in jail!). It was a lovely day, I was "out" and life looked good for the first time in a long while. I thought I would sit in the sun and gradually ease my way back into the community. No such luck.

Little did I realise the furore that Dupas's new charges would bring. When I arrived at the deli, I happened to bump into a great mate of mine, Mark Finnegan, who has been a great support to me all the way through my experience. We sat down in the glorious sun to have a quiet coffee and a catch-up. Just then Mark looked straight over my shoulder and said "Here we go!" I turned around to see a reporter from Channel 9 heading towards me with a camera crew hanging around behind her. I couldn't believe they had found me. I hadn't rung anybody or spoken to anybody about where I was going or what I was doing and it was only after I left Centrelink that I decided to have that coffee. After years in the nick I was enjoying the freedom of being able to do just as I pleased.

At the same time my former wife rang me, distressed that there was a Channel 10 camera crew at her house and that they had harassed my young daughter at the front door. She was very upset and hadn't been able to get out the door to go to school. I asked my ex-wife to get one of the reporters to the phone. A young smartarse told me that as a member of the media he was entitled to be there. I'm not renowned for my subtlety and I told him in no uncertain terms that if he stayed there and went onto my wife's premises one more time I would have him charged with trespass. "Being a member of the media," I told him, "does not give you carte blanche to do what you like and if you don't leave there will be trouble." He then asked a stream of questions, to which I replied "No comment." He said he was going to run the story. I told him that, as I had not answered one question, if he went on the air and made it up, as I anticipated he would, I would sue him personally. The call was very acrimonious, but it turns out Channel 10 left my ex-wife's premises immediately after the phone call, and no story was ever run.

Back at Albert Park, however, Rachael Rollo of Channel 9 wouldn't take no for an answer, so we picked up our coffees from the kerbside table and went inside. The people who own the Albert Park Deli are old friends and said we could use the back door and leave via the back lane. My mate went to get his car and drive it around the back. He immediately rang my mobile and said "Don't bother coming out the back door. Channel 7 have got a crew hanging around the laneway in case you do a runner." I was totally dazed by the media furore that had developed around my release and Dupas being accused. I had, after all, only been out of prison a few hours and suddenly I'd become public property. I'd had no time to re-adjust to the real world.

I decided that I would accept my own advice, the advice I had given to clients many times over the years. Walk straight at the camera, shoulders back, chest out and chin up and look 'em straight in the eye. That way, they get their photo and usually that satisfies them and they go away. Well, that didn't happen on this occasion. There's Ms Rollo tagging along next to me, asking me inane questions, each of which I answered with "No comment." In the end I got so frustrated with her stupidity that I stopped and asked her (this bit was edited out of her report) "What part of no comment do you not understand?" With that, she stopped asking me questions, but it was at that moment that the Channel 9 camera brushed up against me. In jail when somebody touches you unexpectedly you get on the front foot immediately, and purely as a reflex, I nearly hit this guy. I'm glad I didn't. That would have looked just fantastic on TV: day one on parole belting a cameraman! Anyway thank goodness they all went away.

I went home and thought to myself: If this is day one, what's the rest of my time out going to be like? It didn't take long to find out. Later that day a reporter from the *Herald Sun*, Keith Moor, rang me and I had a chat with him. I've known Keith for ages and in my somewhat rattled state, didn't even think that the chat was a 'story'. I was still so upset from all of this media attention that after the conversation I completely forgot I'd had it. My children came to visit and stayed with me for the afternoon and we went out for dinner that night. One thing I have never been able to get over is the amount of publicity my case has generated and continues to generate. After all, I was charged nine years ago and the media still love to mention my transgressions. Hasn't anything else happened in the state of Victoria in the last nine years?

As soon as I was released the Homicide Squad swung into action. Dupas was taken from jail to the Supreme Court where he was directly presented with one count of murdering Mersina Halvagis at the Fawkner Cemetery.

I had placed myself front and centre in one monumental bun fight. I have a well developed sense of the ridiculous and was only too well aware of the irony of my situation: here was Andrew Fraser, the lawyer heaps of coppers loathed and whose demise they had celebrated, now emerging as the Homicide Squad's secret weapon against Dupas. The Homicide Squad had done a terrific job of keeping the lid on my co-operation and I had been released unscathed, no thanks to Fulham and the Office of Corrections. I could not help but ponder the fireworks that would erupt once Dupas was raced into the Supreme Court as I anticipated would happen. I didn't have to wait long for the event!

A direct presentment means that there is no preliminary hearing or committal. A committal is designed to supposedly sift through the evidence and ascertain if there is sufficient evidence that a jury, properly instructed, could return a verdict of guilty. There are, however, provisions to dispense with those proceedings and have the matter taken directly to the Supreme Court for trial – and this is what the Homicide Squad and the Director of Public Prosecutions chose to do. The Halvagis family had done more than enough waiting for justice.

Dupas and his lawyers now had my Can Say Statement, which became public before it was included in the brief. It was now up to me to stick to my word and give evidence against Dupas. The media went into a frenzy. Only recently, after two years out of prison, have the media stopped prefacing my name with "disgraced former lawyer". I became so sick and tired of the epithet that at one stage I was considering changing my name by deed poll to "Disgraced Former Lawyer Andrew Fraser" and saving journalists, particularly Greg Wilkinson of the *Herald Sun* (known in jail as the "Police Gazette" due to its obvious police bias), the bother of using any extra words every time they wrote a story on me. There were huge photos in the papers of me and Dupas, and the electronic media were beside themselves.

The next morning I woke up to see Keith Moor's article as the front page lead in the *Herald Sun*. It drew on our conversation of the day before and it was in lock step with my statement to the police.

The committal proceedings that had been commenced the year before were abandoned once Dupas was directly presented for trial. In cases where additional evidence has come to light after an accused has been committed for trial, a practice has developed in the state of Victoria that allows a pre-trial examination of witnesses before the trial judge. This is called a "Basha inquiry" (after the 1989 case *R v Basha*). It now became apparent that I would have to give evidence in the Supreme Court twice, once at the Basha inquiry and once at the trial proper. This matter was going to trial, come hell or high water!

A trial judge was appointed, His Honour, Mr Justice Phillip Cummins, a most experienced trial judge and one who is awake to every defence and prosecution trick in the book. He is scrupulously fair, even-handed and straight down the line. However, if convicted by him, you invariably receive a large whack.

The furore that greeted my release died down and I was left alone for some time. The Homicide Squad were concerned about how I was travelling and checked on me. I was fine, if still rather shell shocked at the reception I received on release. I started working on my mate's farm in the Otway Ranges, a couple of hours southwest of Melbourne. I was down there on my own, spraying weeds, fencing, helping out shearing and whatever else was required. I loved being there alone, with all the freedom to go into town if I wanted to go and get the papers and to work my own hours, no screws looking over my shoulder and noting my every move. Each day I was waking up very early and I revelled in being able to start work when I felt like it. I would often start at six o'clock in the morning and go through till three or four. Open a bottle of wine and sit out on the balcony and look at the Gellibrand River Valley and think that life wasn't too bad after all.

Jail has affected me in numerous small ways but I only notice these if I go looking for them. For example, before going to jail I couldn't sleep, either during the day or at night, unless the curtains were fully closed. Even a small chink of light peeping in would keep me awake. It didn't really worry me if the window was open or closed. Claustrophobia is something I developed in jail. It was after being banged up in a two-out cell with Andrew Davis for summer that I developed this problem. Our cell was downstairs facing west, with insufficient ventilation, and as a result it was like an oven. Now, before I can sleep, I have to have both the door and the curtains wide open, allowing any available light to pour in.

Jail did seem to leave me more easily shaken, though. One night I was asleep in my house in St Kilda on my own. I didn't have the kids that night. At about one o'clock in the morning, someone started bashing on the front door, ringing the doorbell, bashing again. This went on incessantly for quite some time. I tried to ignore it. In fact, I was so panicked by it that it didn't occur to me to ring the police. Whoever it was would not answer when I yelled out "Who's there?" There was no way I was going to open the front door to see. Who knows what might have happened. I was totally spooked by this incident and finally grabbed the phone and rang the local police. They arrived quickly, to find nobody there. The banging had stopped just as the police car arrived in the vicinity. The coppers interviewed me but it was pointless. I didn't know who it was and I hadn't seen anybody, so I wasn't of much help to them.

The second time I received a visit, it was far worse. As I said, I can't sleep with the curtains or the door closed. The house had a balcony and a very short backyard facing the light rail line that ran from St Kilda to the city and beyond. The view from my balcony looked across the light rail to Albert Park and the city – a beautiful sight indeed, with a huge area of parkland and the lake so close to the CBD. The added bonus was that it was an expansive view, after having been in such cramped confines for so many years. I delighted in just sitting out on the balcony looking, watching people walk their dogs and kids playing cricket, and I started running around the lake everyday. It was fantastic.

However, on this particular night, I was asleep when a beam of light flashed into my bedroom. I thought it was odd because the clock told me it was about three o'clock in the morning, and there are no trams running at that time. I lay dead still and looked across the balcony to my back fence and the light rail. I could see somebody standing on the rail of my back fence shining a torch into the backyard. It was not an indiscriminate flicking around of a torch; the person holding the torch was moving it methodically almost in a grid pattern over the backyard and across the back of the house, as if looking for somewhere to get in. I was scared stiff. However, as there was only one bloke, I barged in where angels fear to tread and raced out onto the balcony, yelling "Oi, you. Fuck off!" The bloke didn't move a muscle. He looked straight up at me but I couldn't see his face. Then I realised he was hooded – not a good omen. With that, two more blokes stepped out from behind a bush. They both had hoods on as well. All three of them stood with their arms crossed, looking straight at me. Nobody said a word but I was clearly being given a message. I don't think I have ever had such a fright, including all the time I spent in jail. I nearly fainted.

That night I had my son, who was fifteen at the time, and my daughter, who was thirteen, sleeping over, with three of my daughter's girlfriends. I was beside myself with fear. I grabbed the phone and went to the linen press, closed the door and rang the coppers. I didn't want the light from the phone screen to signal to these people what I was doing. I then crept back into bed and saw that they were still standing there. After a few minutes, the three of them stepped back and walked towards the city along the light rail. Not hurrying, not looking back, just walking.

I thought: Thank Christ for that – they are gone. I went into the bathroom, which faced away from the light rail line and overlooked the main road running parallel to it. I glanced out the window and couldn't believe my eyes. There were the same three hooded men coming back from the

TAKE A DEEP BREATH: THE PRELIMINARY HEARING

direction in which they had left my house. They had clearly walked up to the first light rail station, exited and walked back down Canterbury Road. They were now standing under a light in the small park directly opposite my house. All standing there with their arms folded.

Even in jail, I never thought I was going to be killed. On this night I did. I thought to myself: Andrew, you are now about to find out what it's like to die. I was scared stiff for the kids in the house. Four teenage girls … what would befall them should these men break in. The front door was deadlocked but it would be nothing against three blokes wanting to kick it in and I had no protection other than a carving knife. Not much of a weapon against three blokes who may or may not have been armed.

Where are the coppers? I rang over half an hour ago and still no appearance. The Homicide Squad had assured me that the local police station at St Kilda had been told I was to be given priority if I rang, and if there was any drama all stops would be pulled out to ensure my safety. If this was how priority looked, I didn't like it much. The men continued to stand with their arms folded, staring straight at my house. I didn't know what to do. Thirty, thirty-five, forty minutes had gone by before the coppers finally arrived. As the police pulled up outside the house, the men just turned and walked off slowly towards the beach, never to be seen again. The police jumped back in their patrol car and drove around the streets and, what a surprise, found nothing. All I could say by way of description was their height and their build and that they appeared to walk as younger men – somewhere, I would say, in their twenties.

Don't think that because blokes are locked up that they can't have a go at you. It's not hard to organise a mate or three on the outside to give someone a going over.

The next morning the Homicide Squad arrived and Paul Scarlett was unamused, to say the least, that it had taken so long for the local coppers to arrive. This was now being treated extremely seriously. I had been passively threatened in my home by people who obviously knew where I lived and were obviously sending me a message. No prizes for guessing what the message was. If I gave evidence, I was going to end up in plenty of bother. During the court proceedings these incidents were not referred to because to mention them would have been highly prejudicial to Dupas.

The police wanted to put me into witness protection. I refused. Bugger that for a joke – I had suffered enough confinement and restrictions. Instead they asked me to find other accommodation for the two weeks before I gave evidence at the Basha inquiry. I moved to another suburb on the other side of town and felt like I was in jail all over again. Each day I went home to get clothes, collect mail and go for a run. Each day I rang the local coppers and met them at home. Each time I had to identify myself. They would wait while I went for my run and then they would leave when I left the house. It was like being in jail all over again, with my every move being monitored whether I liked it or not. I understand it was for my own benefit but it badly destabilised me. I stayed at a friend's house until the day of the Basha inquiry.

I had steeled myself for plenty of media coverage but even I was surprised at the size of the media contingent at the Supreme Court the morning I arrived to give evidence. I was also extremely anxious and apprehensive because I knew from years of cross-examining witnesses that the witness box is a very lonely place. You are stuck up there like a cocky on a perch with no one to help you. You stand or fall by your performance and I was under no misapprehension that I was on trial as well as Dupas. This trial was essentially a one-issue trial: believe me, and Dupas was convicted; disbelieve me and demolish me, and he walked. I had better be on my mettle.

At a preliminary hearing, you do not give "evidence in chief". Evidence in chief is where you recite the contents of your statement, usually without reference to your statement or any notes you may have made. It is a memory test, not a search for truth. Cross-examination by Counsel for the defendant is the cross-examination that you always see on TV shows, where some smarty-pants lawyer rips an unsuspecting witness to pieces, reducing them to tears in the witness box.

Before the trial I read my statement over a number of times. There was no real need to because the circumstances surrounding the incidents, together with the incidents disclosed in my statement, were so startling and so shocking that they were burnt into my memory forever, in particular Dupas's pantomime of murdering Mersina Halvagis. Little did I know then that he had told me something that nobody else knew and only the killer could have known: that Mersina had been kneeling when she was attacked from behind. Often the coppers deliberately withhold particular salient pieces of evidence to stop people constructing a trumped-up story to seek any reward that may be on offer. Another incident that was burnt into my mind and will be forever was Dupas standing on my left in the garden at Sirius East shaking and sweating, weighing up the shiv that I had found and repeating to himself "Mersina, Mersina." How could anybody ever forget those incidents? I certainly can't and to this day they come back to haunt me regularly.

The big day arrived. I was asked to wait outside the court while other preliminary witnesses were dealt with, and I can remember standing in the bluestone-flagged courtyard of the Supreme Court in Melbourne looking up to an office building towering over the court building and thinking to myself: Why in heaven's name did I volunteer to do this? I am going to have everything about my case and my past raked over and thrown back in my face.

I can remember feeling physically sick – not scared of being cross-examined but physically sick at having to face Dupas again, because he was going to be in court for the trial, and at having to face the media, who were harsh critics indeed, notwithstanding the fact that I had literally put my life on the line to give this evidence. Some media, like some coppers, delighted in my demise and refused to move on, returning time and again to my past at every opportunity. And they don't let the facts get in the way of a bigoted, factually wrong piece of editorial comment!

My name was called and I walked up to the witness box. The oath was administered. The Crown prosecutor handed me my statement and asked me whether it was true and correct. I said "Yes." He sat down.

It was now time for the defence to cross-examine. I've known the defence barrister, David Drake, since he was a university student – he is a friend of my sister. That didn't deter him for a moment. David, or "Baldrick" as he is jokingly known, was out to make a name for himself by demolishing me. (Drake's nickname comes from the character in the BBC series, *Black Adder*, because Baldrick always has a cunning plan which invariably fails to materialise.)

Baldrick launched into me at a million miles an hour, all indignant that I should have the temerity to give evidence, that I was a liar, a publicity seeker, a gold digger and a generally disreputable piece of work. I was rather relieved at this tirade because it was heading precisely in the direction I had anticipated – there were no surprises. Shouting and gratuitous abuse did not unsettle me one iota.

For many years, in my first incarnation in the legal system, I was a defence lawyer myself and, like Baldrick, could not

LUNATIC SOUP

wait to try to demolish somebody in the witness box. I admit I went too far on occasions and reduced people to tears. I had witnesses jump out of the witness box and race across the court to try and "get" me, before the police wrestled them to the floor. I had a woman faint in the witness box many years ago, and I had another wet her pants. Now I was on the receiving end!

Being a defence lawyer is in fact a bit of a coward's castle. You stand there manufacturing questions you know the witness can't answer and when the witness hesitates you badger them by saying "Answer Yes or No" and try not to give them an opportunity to explain their answer or elaborate on their answer. If you can keep to a yes or no answer, all the better. The first rule of being a barrister is never ask a question you don't know the answer to, and later we will see how critical this is, because Baldrick did ask one question that he did not know the answer to and it ruined any shred of a defence he may have had.

By the same token, it is not easy being defence counsel. You usually have a client whose neck is on the line, and you have a client who reckons he is paying you too much and is generally unhappy about the state of play. You attend court, you have a prosecutor who is not always scrupulously fair with the facts, coppers who are careless with the truth and, often, a judge who doesn't like his/her job. All in all it's a fairly thankless task. And yet, in the scheme of things, it is a very easy job standing there having a free kick at some poor

180

bugger in the witness box who you reckon you can run rings around. You can make fun of them, you can belittle them, you can shout at them, you can suggest they are lying, making their evidence up or anything else that may get them to put a foot wrong. It's quite alright to cross-examine a person to the point where they lose their temper, because if you can get them to do that then they are likely to say something rash which may be beneficial to your client.

This time the boot is on the other foot, there I stood being cross examined by Baldrick up hill and down dale.

The second incarnation for me in the court system was as a defendant in my own criminal trial. Now, while many people would say that is the most stressful, in fact it's not. Yes, you are worried sick about the potential outcome and what penalty may befall you. From the moment the coppers ran in my front door all those years ago I had a very bad feeling about my fate. That feeling of dread was not helped when a now-retired solicitor Chris Piesse contacted me warning I might cop a seven with a five. And what I did cop? You guessed it: a seven with a five!

When you are a defendant Counsel appears on your behalf and a solicitor acts for you. All this is designed to insulate you from all that is swirling about you in the court room and outside. Even to the point where you don't make statements to the media – your legal team does. You sit tight, say nothing, look suitably admonished and that's about it. Where I had to sit in the court, I couldn't even hear properly what was going on at the front of the court, save to say that there were no prizes for guessing that the judge was clearly unimpressed with me and my co-accused, particularly as it was a drug case. My counsel, Con Heliotis QC, even made submissions that were factually wrong and I was powerless to correct them from where I was sitting at the back of the court.

One contentious issue that continues to cross my mind in these cases and has done so on many occasions is whether a judge in such a trial should declare his or her position as to drugs. For instance, if a judge has a son who has a drug problem, is that relevant to him or her sentencing and the question of his impartiality? Does it affect the quantum of their sentencing? Does it affect their attitude to drugs? Does it affect criminals generally? Does that judge conduct a trial differently? No doubt the judge's little helper, otherwise known as the judge's handbook, will help there! What if a judge has had a brother die of a drug overdose? Should that be declared to the court? I've always found this concept worrying. I think that the answer is "Yes". Judges should declare such issues. For instance, before dealing with a culpable driver they should declare if they have had a loved one killed or maimed in a car accident. Or before dealing with an armed robber they should declare whether they have been in a bank when it was robbed. These are all examples of how judges are human and are subject to human frailty and prejudice. I know for a fact that a couple of these examples have arisen and not a squeak was uttered.

Sitting there in my own case, I took a keen interest in proceedings but everything was being done for me. This was, believe it or not, the easiest of the three roles in which I have found myself. Easily the most distressing and difficult was being a Crown witness. But not just any Crown witness. Upon Dupas's direct presentment, the then Director of Public Prosecutions, His Honour Mr Justice Coghlan, described my evidence as "the coat rack by which all other coats hang; no coat rack, no coats". In other words, without me there was no case against Dupas. Therefore, for Dupas to be acquitted, I had to be demolished in the witness box. I knew that, the prosecution knew that and it was bleedin' obvious to the defence. I steeled myself for the onslaught, which inevitably came. Be under no misapprehension: Peter Dupas was on trial for murder but I was on trial as well. My entire credibility, which I had worked hard to re-establish after my sentence and for the few months since I had been released, was on trial. I had plenty to lose should I not be believed. However, for Dupas to be convicted, I had to be believed by the jury and that was yet to come.

I made a mistake in my cross-examination with Baldrick on the Basha inquiry when I said I had not spoken to any newspaper people when I was first released. As I have already said, I did speak to Keith Moor and had forgotten that. Yes, forgotten; not deliberately hidden or omitted.

As things transpired, the Basha inquiry went according to plan and I felt reasonably comfortable in the witness box. Needless to say it was the full court room drama with robes, wigs, the judge and barristers. Only the jury was missing. There were certainly no surprises and not much dirt was thrown at me. At the conclusion of the Basha inquiry the matter was adjourned for the trial. The procedure is that a written transcript is made of all of the evidence given at the Basha and this is given to all parties. The transcript is particularly of benefit to the defence because then they can see whether there are any inconsistencies between the written evidence in the form of the statement and the oral evidence given at the Basha inquiry.

Committal proceedings are a vexed question in the law and it is my view that they are a complete and utter waste of time. A lot of the trial is a waste of time as well. It is a constant bone of contention in the media and in law reform commissions how the cost and the length of trials have blown out in the last fifteen or twenty years. Once upon a time a murder trial went for a week; now they can go for months. There is too much waffle and most of the time-wasting is caused by inexperienced and/or gutless judges who fail to intervene; they allow the most experienced counsel, who are usually the main offenders, to question witnesses around and around in circles and to keep asking the same question multiple different ways. The old adage is that the question doesn't get any better for the repetition, nor does the answer. Counsel is stuck with an answer a witness gives, so you need to be very careful how you pose a question!

In trials, the only thing that matters is the sworn evidence of the witnesses and, if called, the accused, and their cross-examination. To understand this better, let's have a look at the basics of how a trial runs.

Jury selection takes place. These days this can take some considerable time because, if the trial is a sensational one, people might say the media coverage has caused them to form a view likely to be prejudicial to the accused. These people are always excused. Also people who are sick or infirm or who have pressing business engagements or child commitments are usually excused as well.

Once a jury has finally been selected, an opening by the Crown prosecutor outlines the case from the Crown's point of view and this too can go for a very long time. Following the Crown's opening, the defence opening outlines the case from the defence's perspective and how the defence will run its case.

Then comes the trial proper. This is where all sworn evidence and cross-examination of witnesses take place. Once the evidence is concluded the Crown sums up the prosecution's case. This is called a final address. The defence also gets to make a final address to the jury. After the final addresses comes the judge's charge to the jury. The judge has a lash at reiterating the facts for a third time just in case the jury have not understood plain English. The learned trial judge charges the jury as to the law. During this aspect of the trial the jury is obliged to listen and apply the law according to the judge's direction.

The jury then retires to consider its verdict according to the evidence. Remember that in our legal system the jury is the only arbiter of the facts, so it is logical that they need to listen to the facts and only the facts.

In all of this, there are only two aspects of which the jury is obliged at law to take any notice: the sworn evidence together with cross-examination, and the judge's charge as to the law. A juror can, if they like, go to sleep or stare at the ceiling. They do not have to take notice of any of the other stuff that is said in court, so all the waffle of addresses becomes so much hot air. Everybody dances around this issue and nobody is prepared to meet it head-on. But the fact of the matter is that lawyers stand up and waffle for five-sevenths of the trial, none of which the jury is required to take the slightest bit of notice of. Why do we have a Crown opening? Why do we have a defence opening? Why do we have a Crown closing? Why do we have a defence closing? Well, it's very simple. It is the skill of the barrister that gets you across the line in most jury cases. There is no doubt about it: the better the counsel, the better your chances of a good result. The old adage of paying peanuts to get monkeys is never truer than in a criminal trial. Philip Dunn QC is an old friend and a skilled advocate as well as a terrific raconteur. Philip always says "Justice is something you get when your money runs out!" Very funny but also true.

Recently, in this state, there was a trial of a man who was charged with very serious crimes and briefed Robert Richter QC to appear on his behalf. The Crown did not take the advice given to it to brief a senior prosecutor and instead briefed a more junior prosecutor, notwithstanding that he was senior counsel. Robert Richter is probably one of the best half dozen trial lawyers in this country and consequently made mince meat of the Crown prosecutor. The result: the defendant was convicted of a much lesser penalty. The community and media were in uproar over this result. The fact is that Richter is good and apparently on this trial he was at his absolute best, convincing the jury by sheer power of speech to accept his version of events. That is not, with all due respect to Robert Richter, judging a case on its merits. The jury was clearly convinced by a super salesman – which is, after all, what barristers are.

Therefore, if we want to shorten criminal trials and stop juries being bamboozled ("if you can't dazzle them with brilliance, baffle them with bullshit"), then the two openings and the two closings, together with the judge's summing up of the facts, should all be dispensed with. Impanel a jury, have the evidence and have the judge charge as to the law. Everything else is superfluous and wastes time and money. Committal proceedings are in the same boat. All committals do is give the defence another free kick at a witness, and you have all the statements that witness made to the police, plus what is said in the witness box at the committal proceedings, plus the cross-examination at the committal proceedings. You can then sit there and compare and contrast all of the evidence and it's amazing how many inconsistencies, albeit small, that you find in that evidence. On trial, stand up and painstakingly take any witness through each and every inconsistency or contradiction and try to blow it out of all proportion. That's your job, that's what you do. But it is most certainly not having the jury decide the issues on the facts and the evidence alone.

The long and short of it all is that, in my view, drastic trial reform is long overdue. Of course all those with a vested interest will say that is not right; but the reality is that nobody is required to listen to one word except the sworn evidence and the judge's charge as to the law, so why have the rest? The answer is inescapable. It ought be abolished.

Justice, if delivered properly, is a relatively simple, quick and cheap way of deciding on disputes between people or between the state and an individual for a transgression of the law. King John signed the Magna Carta at Runnymede to establish a justice system that was accessible to all. Unfortunately, since then, economic rationalism has largely taken over. Local courts have been closed, so justice is no longer taken to the people; rather, the people must come to the justice – the exact opposite of King John's thinking. What has happened to our most basic of rights? On the other side of the coin, trials in superior courts have been allowed to blow out and drag on at infinitum.

My cross-examination at the Basha had lasted only a few hours and I emerged unscathed. But I knew that this was only a test run for the trial proper and that Baldrick would be keeping his powder dry on a few issues in order to try to surprise me when next we met.

Chapter 12

The Trial: Not a Nice Day at the Office

That he which has no stomach to this fight, let him depart.

– WILLIAM SHAKESPEARE, *HENRY V*

The Basha inquiry had hardly concluded when, on my daily run around Albert Park Lake, I realised that I had in fact had a conversation with Keith Moor immediately after my release and that he had written the story up but in the shock of the new I had forgotten about this. There had been so much to adjust to and catch up with, a lot that happened in those first few days was a blur. But this was no big deal. People do forget and are allowed to forget. It doesn't mean they are lying, notwithstanding what a defence lawyer might assert.

THE TRIAL: NOT A NICE DAY AT THE OFFICE

I immediately contacted Senior Detective Scarlett and told him of my oversight. He was not particularly perturbed about it either and said it would no doubt be a matter of some heated cross-examination at the trial – which I knew to be highly likely because if I had been the defence counsel I would have been onto this point like a shot. I would have been carrying on that it was all a lie, a fabrication, I'd made it up, I was chasing the reward, and anything else that I could think of to discredit me. And so it was to be!

Now that the Basha inquiry was out of the way I returned home. I am pleased to say there were no further incidents because once you have given your sworn evidence, even if you are "brown bread" (dead) or no longer around, that evidence can later be used at the trial as your evidence.

After many anxious moments and sleepless nights, the day of the trial arrived. I realised again how much the jail experience had changed me. The thought of seeing Dupas again made me feel physically ill. I wanted more than anything not to have to endure this experience again but I knew there was no escape from my obligations. I had purposely not read anything about the trial in the media and as I hardly ever watch commercial television I hadn't seen any of those news services, which apparently gave the case blanket coverage.

I knew I was going to be in for a torrid time in the witness box and as a result I slept particularly badly the night before. It's funny how life changes. Once upon a time, going to court was like water off a duck's back to me. It's something I did – all day, every day – for a living. Yes, you get nervous, but it's the kind of nervousness you might feel before a race or a football match. It's a good nervousness: it helps you perform at your best. The nervousness I felt the night before the trial and as I was heading to court was different: it was a feeling of dread. It took me back to my brief time as a defendant and what it subsequently lead to, not to the great days when I was practising as a lawyer. Funnily enough, the last matter over which I had appeared in the Supreme Court as a lawyer was a manslaughter case and it was before His Honour, Mr Justice Philip Cummins the judge on this case. Another one of life's little parallels.

At the Basha inquiry I had purposely not spoken to the Halvagis family, but when I arrived at court for the trial the look of sheer desolation and deep sorrow on the faces of the entire family was gut wrenching. I don't think I have ever seen anybody more devastated by a bereavement than George Halvagis. As he walked towards me in the hallway outside the court, I merely extended my hand to him. At the same time I kept walking and did not say a word to him. I was not giving Baldrick any ammunition if I could possibly help it.

It must be said that this prosecution had come about almost exclusively because of the efforts of George Halvagis and his family. He refused to let go of the fact that his daughter had been murdered and he wanted some answers –

he wanted closure. He had been single-minded in his purpose since the day of Mersina's murder. He petitioned the government, constantly kept in touch with police as to developments and was vocal in the Victims of Crime organisation.

Until the police contacted me and I came forward, there was insufficient evidence to prove Dupas had murdered Mersina. It was well known in police circles, and well known to the Halvagises, that Dupas was the man responsible but at law knowledge is insufficient to constitute proof. Hard evidence that has been tested under cross-examination is the acid test of whether an accused is guilty beyond all reasonable doubt.

The Halvagis family are typical of the post-war European migrant families that have made our multi-cultural society so great. The Halvagises have a wonderful work ethic and they had worked hard to establish themselves and be successful in Australia. The same work ethic had been instilled in Mersina. She was engaged to be married and had bought a house. By another of life's coincidences, she had a part-time job working for a friend of mine in one of his service stations at Nunawading. She worked there as a console operator, and when my friend found out that I was giving evidence in the prosecution of Dupas he volunteered to me what a wonderful person Mersina had been. She was good with the customers, hard working, honest, a delight to have at his workplace. Everyone loved her, and my friend's final comment about her was: "She was the type of employee that every employer aspires to have work for him."

On the day of her murder Mersina had visited Fawkner Cemetery to tend her grandmother's grave, another example of the sort of person she was. She would often put flowers on graves that appeared unkempt because she couldn't stand the thought of those people being interred there with nobody caring for them.

The trial began in a blaze of publicity. I stayed away from the Supreme Court until it was my turn in the hot seat. Paul Scarlett gave me a couple of hours' notice of roughly the time I would be facing the music.

I was not the first witness called in this trial, and there had been a substantial body of evidence given by the time I reached the witness box. One thing I did see in the media was that an identification witness has come forward with evidence about a person who had stalked her at the Fawkner Cemetery at about the time when Mersina had been murdered and this witness prepared a photofit identification with the police. A photofit is a process whereby you sit in front of a computer and an operator constructs the shape of the face, the type and colour of hair, glasses if any, shape of the nose, all the facial features until you have somebody you say looks like the offender.

When I picked up the newspaper the morning after the identification witness's evidence I nearly fell over. Looking back at me from the front page was Peter Dupas. Not a question of *degree* of likeness; it was him! It was the best and strongest piece of photofit identification evidence I had ever seen. This woman's recall was extraordinary to say the least, and would have been a big factor in Dupas's conviction. Except for the fact that merely being sighted at the Fawkner Cemetery around the time of the attack was insufficient. It didn't prove that Dupas was the killer and, in the absence of any forensic evidence to corroborate the witness's observations, the prosecution could go nowhere.

When I attended court I was met by Scarlett and ushered into a little ante room outside the court. There I was to sit, trying to read the paper (without success because I was too nervous to concentrate), until my name was called. Each day in the countdown to the trial since the Basha inquiry the feeling of dread in me had mounted, and all I wanted now was for it to be over.

People had warned me that this was going to be difficult. They asked if I really wanted to go ahead with it and have a bucket load of shit poured on me but I gave my word and I was determined to follow through. I was always taught to confront the issue. The day will come and the day will go – better to face the music and get on with it.

"Call Andrew Roderick Fraser!" called the tipstaff (judge's assistant). Here we go young fella, once more unto the breach, dear friend, once more! This is it, Sydney or the bush!

The Supreme Court of Victoria is a classic, imposing Victorian Building constructed along the lines of the

Supreme Court in Dublin, Ireland. It was built in the 1800s
when Queen Victoria was still on the throne of England.
With Victoria at the end of the great gold rush, and
colonial confidence high, imposing buildings for posterity
was the order of the day. The court was constructed to
preserve the sanctity and solemnity of the law and was
designed with another objective: to scare the living
daylights out of those appearing therein. The effect persists
to this day!

The design of each court room is deliberately intimidating.
After my name was called I walked onto the floor of the
court, which is the lowest point. Immediately to my left,
only a couple of metres away, was the dock – sitting higher
than the floor where the lawyers sit but not as high as the
jury and witness boxes. His Honour the learned trial judge
sits at the highest point in the room. Walking this close to
Dupas was intimidating and frankly unnecessary; I could
have been brought in via the side door. Seeing Dupas sitting
there wearing his usual Sphinx-like visage was unsettling.
There he was, fatter, with the same blank, denying face, the
blinds down in his cold, calculating eyes, just as I had seen
them many times while banged up with him.

I gathered myself as best I could, paused and bowed to
His Honour, who smiled at me and bowed in return. I
wonder what he thought of this little effort by young
Andrew. After all, I had appeared before him numerous
times over the years and here I was now, a convicted criminal

and pivotal Crown witness. Some day maybe I will find out what he made of me.

Sitting in the witness box I didn't look at the accused, who is sitting at the back of the court. I could see Dupas out of the corner of my eye, but not once did I look at him. Also, I didn't look much at defence counsel or the prosecutor who was conducting evidence in chief. I looked across the court from my high perch in the witness box, past the trial judge, straight at the jury, because they are the only people in the court who matter. They were the ones who I wanted to believe my evidence. From the point of view of convicting or acquitting the accused, it is the jury – not the judge, not the defence counsel, not the prosecution – that counts.

The prosecutor was Colin Hillman SC to whom I had been opposed many times over the years. Colin is a most experienced and competent prosecutor, even if we had not seen eye to eye on many occasions. It felt odd to me, and no doubt to Colin, that we were both pushing in the same direction for once – and not only that, we were polite to each other!

His Honour, Mr Justice Philip Cummins – known in the legal profession as "Fabulous Phil", or "Fabbo" for short – is, as I have said, one of the most experienced trial judges sitting in the state of Victoria. What his honour does not know about criminal trials is not worth knowing. Fabbo is a no-nonsense judge who does not waste time and is blunt if he thinks counsel are doing just that. His trials are run fairly, straight down the line, but (as I've said) heaven help you if you are convicted and Fabbo sentences you; you will invariably cop a big whack. This is another aspect of the profession I have pondered over the years: why do some judges, who were once predominately defence advocates pleading for leniency, often turn out to be the heaviest hitters in sentencing once they are appointed to the bench? I have also seen former Crown prosecutors who become positively benevolent in their sentencing after years of prosecuting.

The defence team of David Drake and Mark Regan had the most unenviable task. As defence counsel you do not have to believe, or for that matter like, your client but you are duty bound to follow your client's lawful instructions, even if you think those instructions are nonsense. You cannot make things up. Both were briefed by Legal Aid, who invariably end up acting for blokes like Dupas. Drake or Baldrick as he is known in legal circles had a cunning plan to discredit me; however I never did work out precisely what that plan was, apart from calling me a liar.

As I made the long walk from court door to my lofty perch in the witness box I was careful to keep my eyes straight ahead and under no circumstances make eye contact with either Dupas or the Halvagis family. I was indeed following the advice that I had given hundreds of clients. Take the oath and look directly across the court, directly at the jury, each in turn. Watch the jury's body language and try to make sure they listen to your answers; after all, it is the answers and not the questions that form the evidence. It is the jury alone who will decide the fate of the accused; the judge merely passes sentence after conviction.

As I said earlier, during the Basha inquiry I had forgotten all about my discussion with Keith Moor, the reporter from the *Herald Sun*, but immediately, under cross-examination, I acknowledged having had that conversation and the fact that I had forgotten it. Baldrick, instead of then just saying that I had made the whole thing up and I was lying, went through each and every sentence in that article, putting to me that each one was a lie. My answer each time: "No, I forgot." One thing he didn't do was look at my Can Say Statement and compare it with the article in the *Herald Sun*; if he had, he would have seen that they were factually identical – there was not one inconsistency.

Baldrick made the fundamental and fatal error for any counsel in a jury trial of turning his back on the jury. This was his usual method of cross-examination: to turn his back to the jury, lean on the lectern and sneer at the witness. In my book he failed the most fundamental lesson: always play to the jury! The jury may as well not have been in the court. The only time Baldrick looked at the jury throughout the entire trial, I have been informed, was during his closing address. By then it was too late: he had lost the jury. I was watching the jury. As he laboured the same question over and over and over again throughout what was quite a lengthy newspaper article, the members of the jury were starting to roll their eyes, they were yawning, they were fidgeting, they were bored and their body language indicated that they weren't interested in any of this questioning. But Baldrick didn't twig because his back was turned to the jury.

Apart from this line of questioning Baldrick had nothing else to put to me, except to suggest that I had been using drugs while I made these statements to the police, because they were, in his view, so fanciful. There was one problem with that contention. After I was charged on the 13 September 1999 I ceased using and had been subject to repeated random drug testing by my general practitioner for the two years that I was on bail. I was then subject to random drug testing while I was in jail. Since my release from jail on 11 September 2006 I had been on parole, and while on parole I was also subject to random drug testing. I don't know how many times I have been drug tested, but it is many, and needless to say I have not returned one positive sample. All of this was on the record as a clear rebuttal of Baldrick's contention.

I was adamant with the Crown prosecutor that, on re-examination (which follows cross-examination), I wanted an opportunity to answer the question as to whether I was on drugs as Baldrick had asserted.

When the Crown prosecutor did start to re-examine me Baldrick jumped up and down, objecting to the question, saying it was irrelevant whether I had been taking drugs.

The trial judge reminded him that he had opened that particular can of worms, so he could wear the answers given in re-examination. I was then able to explain to the jury how long it was since I had used drugs and that the suggestion that I had been using was nothing more than a deliberate slur.

As I said earlier, the police had not made public the fact that Mersina Halvagis had been kneeling when she was attacked from behind. When I described that posture to the police there was only one way I could have known of it, and that was from the killer personally. As it transpired, forensic evidence disclosed that Mersina had been stabbed a couple of times in the shoulder region of the upper body and the majority of stab wounds were concentrated in the breast area.

Baldrick put it to me that I must be lying about Mersina Halvagis kneeling because the stab wounds were in the chest area. I said any statement by me about chest wounds would be speculation. He then barked at me to answer the question. I can clearly remember saying "If you want me to speculate I can easily tell you what's happened." I then went on to say that, from what Dupas had re-enacted to me, the deceased was kneeling, she was small, she was attacked with great force from behind, the first couple of blows struck her in the neck or upper shoulder area, the sheer force of these blows had made her fall her backwards and she was then stabbed repeatedly in the chest. This was exactly what Baldrick did not want to hear and he tried desperately to stop me. I was looking at the jury. Their eyes were out on stalks. The trial judge refused to stop me, on the basis that Baldrick had asked the question and had pursued an answer and he was now stuck with the contents of that answer.

Clearly the most telling piece of evidence, in the eyes of the jury, was the incident in Dupas's cell that I have already outlined. I was asked in evidence in chief by Colin Hillman SC, the Crown prosecutor, to re-enact the pantomime for the jury. I left the witness box and went down to the body of the court and re-enacted the incident where Dupas had acted out for me the stabbing of Mersina. I was watching the jury the entire time I was carrying out this pantomime. I had their complete attention – they were enthralled. One woman, who was sitting in the front row of the jury, was particularly shocked by this – I could tell by the look on her face.

I then went on to talk about finding the knife in the garden and watching Dupas weighing it up in his hand and repeating "Mersina, Mersina". The same juror was clearly horrified at that.

My cross-examination had lasted nearly three days and had been long and boring, and that was obviously the impact it had had on the jury.

Dupas's defence had boiled down to one thing: an allegation repeated ad nauseam that I lied at the Basha, that I was a gold digger, a publicity hound and a general bullshit artist. Not one shred of evidence to rebut any aspect of my sworn testimony was led by the defence, and accordingly there was not a conflicting point of view the jury could consider.

As the accused Dupas was not required to say anything in his defence. However, if the accused doesn't, then that fact can be highlighted in the Crown's final address to the jury. In other words, it is quite acceptable for the judge to observe that the accused has chosen not to give evidence in his own defence. Of course, Dupas would not go anywhere near the witness box because he would risk bringing himself undone by lying. The defence called no witnesses whatsoever.

After a three-and-a-half-week trial the jury retired to consider its verdict. A few days later I received a phone call from Paul Scarlett to say "The matter is over: Dupas has been convicted." I didn't realise how much impact this trial had had on me until I had heard those words: "He has been convicted." I put the phone down and burst into tears. I had not been sleeping well. I had been having, and continued to have, a recurring nightmare. In it Dupas escapes from prison and he comes looking for me. He is never front and centre in the dream, he is always somewhere in the crowd and I just catch glimpses of his face, but he is always there, that silent, ever-present malevolence.

I withstood a huge barrage of attacks from the media but it motivated me more to do what I consider to be the right thing. People warned me that the media would sensationalise the trial and it was hard – especially with teenage kids and trying to rebuild my life. It was hard to keep my head in a good space. But my parents set an example of honesty that was ingrained in me.

While I was in the witness box my manager, Victor Susman, was present in the body of the court, watching. Halfway through the cross-examination, Mersina's brother approached him and told him that the family was deeply grateful for my bravery, for the fact that I had been gutsy enough to come forward and tell the truth. It was when Victor told me this that I confirmed in my own mind that I was definitely doing the right thing, because these people needed finalisation.

Once Dupas had been convicted and been sentenced to a third life term without parole, the new hot topic was the reward offered by the state government, a substantial one million dollars. Everybody seemed interested in whether I should get the reward given that I had been in jail and that was the only way I had obtained the incriminating evidence. Well, like it or not, the people who are going to have evidence that a reward might flush out aren't usually little old ladies who work on a volunteer basis in the local opportunity shop. Most of the witnesses who claim rewards are crooks who have criminal records and have been in jail. Why? Because they are the people who talk to other criminals and to whom other criminals often make voluntary admissions that return to bite them some time in the future.

I would never have received the admissions from Dupas if, for instance, I had visited him on a professional basis in jail, or by being his lawyer for any other matter. He is that type of person who would never have made those admissions to anyone else. The very fact that it had taken some months of me working in the garden with him, and the coincidence of timing that I was with him in jail at the time of the Margaret Maher and Mersina Halvagis investigations that he let his guard down sufficiently to make the admissions to me, was significant.

Time and time again over the years the coppers have had Dupas in custody and questioned him, and every time he has behaved in exactly the manner I described to them. They didn't describe it to *me*; I told *them*. And it was only after I had made my formal statement that the police told me that over the years Dupas's behaviour has been totally consistent. That is, he sits in a police station being interviewed, he gets to a stage where you think he is going to make admissions, he starts sweating and becomes nervous, anxious and shaky, then clasps his hands together. Then, when he is really anxious, he puts his hands between his legs and crushes his knees together and then starts rocking backwards and forwards. Every other time he has displayed those behaviours he has pulled himself up short and that has been the end of the discussion. The blinds come down and he blocks the matter out of his mind and he will not talk about it any more. The only difference, with me, was that he took the process one step further and blurted out the admissions that led to his conviction. It was only after he had blurted out the admissions that the blinds came down. Not much of a change, but a change of immense significance as far as the police, the Halvagis family and the Victorian public were concerned.

As I said earlier, being in the witness box was easily the most disturbing thing I have ever done; and frankly, if I knew then what I know now, I wonder whether I would have come forward to give the evidence when requested. However, now that it's done and Dupas is convicted, I am pleased that I have come through the ordeal and this poor family now has some closure.

Mr and Mrs Halvagis visit their daughter's grave daily. These people have been devastated by what happened to them and I, as a parent, can understand that to lose a child would be the most horrible thing that could happen to you. But to lose such a beautiful child in such tragic circumstances is something you would never recover from. I am told by people who have been to the Halvagis family home that Mersina's bedroom has not been touched since the day she was murdered. It is almost a shrine to her. These are good people who came to a new country to provide their kids with something they would never have had if they had stayed in Greece – and this is what they get. I am glad I did what I did.

Chapter 13

What Else? Solved and Unsolved Atrocities

Science is always simple and always profound, it is only the half truths that are dangerous.

– GEORGE BERNARD SHAW, *THE DOCTOR'S DILEMMA*

Peter Dupas was the prime suspect in six murders. He has now been convicted of three of those and he is serving three life sentences without any prospect of parole.

Nicole Amanda Patterson

Dupas was suspected, and eventually convicted, of the murder of Nicole Patterson on 19 April 1999 after her semi-naked body was found lying on the lounge-room floor of her home in the northern Melbourne suburb of Northcote. She had been stabbed twenty-seven times and both of her breasts had been removed after death.

When the Homicide Squad arrived at the scene they found that the killer had removed jewellery and other items from her body and worn them. The killer had also removed her shirt and had taken that and unknown bloodied items, most likely the victim's breasts, down to her bedroom where there is further evidence that the killer has dressed up in the victim's clothing.

There was further evidence that the killer had searched the victim's premises before leaving, clearly with a view to finding any incriminating evidence. However, the killer missed one most important item, and that was Nicole's diary. On the day of her death she had written "Malcolm 9.00 am" and a phone number. A call charge record on the deceased's phone revealed that a number which belonged to Dupas, who was by then a convicted serial rapist with a propensity for violence, had called Miss Patterson fifteen times over the last week, a chilling fact indeed.

Not long after, on 22 April, Homicide Squad detectives arrested Dupas at a local hotel and searched his house. In the rubbish bin outside the house police found a pair of white runners with blood stains all over them. Also located was a small piece of newspaper that had been torn into several pieces. When pieced back together, this piece of paper revealed the handwritten note "Nicci – Northcote – 9.00 o'clock morning – Malcolm". It is obvious now that

Dupas had rung and used a false name for the purposes of making an appointment with the victim. Also, on his fridge, was a handwritten note with a mobile number: the same as the phone number written in Patterson's diary. Dupas had obviously deviously used another mobile phone to ring Patterson and make his fatal appointment.

During their search of the premises, the police also found a copy of the *Herald Sun* with the front page showing Patterson's face after her murder was discovered. The picture had been slashed with a knife. Located in the garage were numerous tools with their handles wrapped in yellow electrical tape; the tape was identical to that found on the deceased's body.

Well hidden in Dupas's garage were a balaclava, gloves and a green army jacket with a packet of condoms in the pocket. On the sleeves were blood stains. DNA testing was later conducted and it became clear that the blood on the runners found in the rubbish bin and the blood on the jacket sleeve as that of Miss Patterson. Dupas was charged and bail refused. This was the beginning of the rest of his life in custody.

At the trial, expert evidence was given that the blood on the jacket located in Dupas's garage was 6.53 billion times more likely to be that of Nicole Patterson than any other person. As a former lawyer familiar with DNA testing, I can say that these sorts of numbers show categorically that the blood was Nicole Patterson's. Floated as Dupas's defence was the highly unlikely and in my view fanciful scenario that Detective Senior Sergeant Geoff Maher and Detective Senior Detective Paul Scarlett had obtained a phial of the deceased's blood and had walked around and sprinkled it liberally all over Dupas's jacket and runners during the execution of the search warrant. I have heard some fanciful defences in my day, but this one takes the cake. It is no wonder the jury only took two hours to convict Dupas, and His Honour Justice Vincent duly sentenced him to life imprisonment with no minimum.

Margaret Josephine Maher

Margaret Maher was a well-known heroin user and had been addicted to the drug for most of her adult life. She had struggled with her use, as is often the case with heroin addicts, and had been unable to support her habit through legal means, so had turned to prostitution – a very common event.

According to discussions I have had with people who knew her, she was considered likeable, harmless and a bit of a hopeless case as far as her drug use and prostitution were concerned. On 4 October 1997 at about 1.45 pm, the body of Margaret Maher was found dumped on the side of Cliffords Road, Somerton. She had been assaulted and stabbed numerous times and her left breast had been severed and shoved into her mouth. The police sealed off the area and began a minute forensic examination of the scene. Located on and near the deceased's body were items of rubbish and discarded computer equipment that had purposely been placed there obviously to conceal the deceased's body from passers-by. A problem for the killer was that one of his woollen gloves had slipped off and was found in the pile of rubbish.

You will note that Margaret Maher's murder took place before Nicole Patterson's. There was an extensive investigation by the Homicide Squad and they couldn't find any records of a killer having severed a breast over the previous ten years. Sexually motivated killers usually follow a pattern of behaviour, whether they mean to or not. Once the pattern has been established, they tend to stick to it pretty rigorously. The only other known murder in which a breast was severed came in April 1999 when Dupas was arrested for the murder of Nicole Patterson. This breakthrough in the investigation was the beginning of the end for Peter Dupas because the Victoria police formed a task force known as Mikado and it re-examined the unsolved murders of five women: Margaret Maher, Mersina Halvagis, Kathleen Downes, Helen McMahon and Renita Brunton.

Having got to know Detective Senior Sergeant Geoff Maher and Detective Senior Constable Paul Scarlett well during my interaction with them and in the course of my giving evidence in the Mersina Halvagis prosecution, I can say from first-hand experience that these two police officers are dedicated, dogged and meticulous in the pursuit of solving outstanding crimes. That was how Senior Detective Scarlett came to talk to me at Fulham about Mersina Halvagis; any other cop would have put the issue of talking to me in the too-hard basket.

The police went back over all of the evidence that had been discovered at the scene and in the case. The obvious item for re-examination was the black woollen glove located alongside the victim's body. DNA techniques have rocketed in their accuracy in the last decade or so, and the woollen glove was again subjected to DNA investigation, but this time using the most recent and accurate of testings. A DNA sample was subsequently discovered inside the glove, and Dupas could not be excluded as the source of this sample.

In a great piece of lateral thinking the coppers went back over Dupas's phone records around the time of the death of Maher, and found that calls had been made from his landline to a phone sex service known as "Grandma's sex line" on 1 November 1997, the day Dupas murdered Mersina Halvagis, and not quite a month since he had murdered Margaret Maher. The police spoke to a phone sex operator who was clearly rattled by the person who had called that day. She remembered a male calling the line and detailing to her how he had cut off a woman's breast and cut around the nipple. She further recalled how the anonymous caller appeared to become more sexually aroused as he spoke about blood pouring over his knife and referred to the victim as his mother, "the bitch!" The person on the other end of the phone described in great detail injuries that bore a striking resemblance to the post-mortem injuries inflicted by Dupas on Margaret Maher.

On 2 October 2002 Dupas was charged with Maher's murder and after a three-week trial he was convicted and sentenced to a second life sentence.

Mersina Halvagis

On Saturday 1 November 1997 Mersina left her fiancé's house and drove to the Fawkner Cemetery to tend her grandmother's grave, as was her usual practice. She arrived at the cemetery at about 3.30 pm and was last seen alive walking away from the car park at the Greek Orthodox section of the cemetery towards her grandmother's grave. Mersina failed to arrive home that afternoon, and by that evening an extensive search involving all of her family and her fiancé was underway. It was totally out of character for her not to be at home on time. At about 4.00 am the following morning, Mersina's fiancé climbed over the boundary fence into the cemetery. Lying in an empty plot just two graves from her grandmother's gravesite, he made the gruesome discovery of Mersina's body.

The Homicide Squad was called to the scene of the grisly murder. It was apparently random and obviously carried out with great force, displaying the frenzied infliction of a great number of wounds. The scene indicated to the police that Mersina had fought courageously with her attacker, despite the fact that she was short and weighed just 55 kilograms. A significant injury to the back of her head indicated that she had been attacked from behind, and she had received over eighty stab wounds to her body, with an obvious concentration in the breast area. The similarity with the Patterson and Maher murders was marked.

Unlike in the case of Margaret Maher, however, there was no glove containing a DNA sample at the scene; and unlike Patterson, no phone records to connect anybody to the murder. This attack appeared to be truly random – until it later emerged that Dupas's grandmother is buried within a couple of hundred metres of Mersina's grandmother. So much for Dupas's later assertion that he had no connection to Fawkner Cemetery, had no knowledge of the area and had no logical reason to be there. Again deny, deny, deny.

The Halvagis family were devastated and constantly kept at everybody concerned to try to solve this awful murder. One of the most touching aspects of this investigation from the police's point of view was the unflinching love of the family for their deceased daughter and sister and their unyielding determination to have Mersina's killer brought to justice. Meanwhile, there was not one skerrick of forensic evidence for the police to hang their hat on. Over the next couple of years the police investigated, and eliminated as persons of interest, 215 suspects and they obtained 149 statements.

While the police were minutely combing whatever evidence they could find, it became apparent to them that, in the five months leading up to Mersina's murder, there had been seven separate instances of females being approached at the Fawkner Cemetery, sometimes aggressively, by an unknown male. A couple of the women got a very good look at his face. When Dupas was apprehended for Nicole Patterson's murder and his photograph was shown in the media, several women contacted police to say that he was the man who had accosted them in the cemetery. There are always problems with identification evidence, particularly after a long period of time, but Dupas's face is quite distinctive, particularly as he is an older man, making it the kind that can be easily identified.

In May 2005 the police contacted me and I provided them with the evidence that was required to charge Dupas. He pleaded Not Guilty. The case received a huge amount of media coverage and, on 27 August 2007, Dupas was convicted of his second murder. He was again sentenced to life, no minimum.

The above three murders are those we know Dupas has committed. What about those for which he has never been convicted?

Helen McMahon

It is believed that Helen McMahon may have been Dupas's first victim. On 13 February 1985 she left the Willows Caravan Park where she was living at Rosebud, in coastal Victoria, and went to the nearby Rye back beach. From the car park she walked about 800 metres into the sand dunes. For those of you who know this area, it is semi National Park Coastal Reserve, deserted and covered with very large sand dunes, which affords privacy and quiet. Helen McMahon liked this area because it was her habit to sunbake nude and it provided the isolation she required. What probably ended up being her undoing was the fact that she always went to sunbake in the same place, making her easy prey for a stalker.

At about 3.30 pm on that afternoon a passer-by noticed McMahon lying naked and partially wrapped in a towel. At first the person who saw the body thought nothing much of it until he noticed that the towel covering her was blood soaked and the surrounding sand was covered in blood. The passer-by then realised McMahon was dead and reported his gruesome discovery to the Rye police.

A police pathologist who conducted a post mortem said that McMahon died as a result of inter-cranial haemorrhage and contusions resulting from multiple blows to the head. There was also bruising on her hands which suggests that she was trying to protect herself during this violent and obviously unprovoked attack. When the crime scene examiners went over the area with a fine-toothed comb they found, among other things, a piece of blood-splattered wooden stake next to the naked body.

At the time of McMahon's death Dupas was serving a twelve-year sentence for rape, so how could he possibly be in the frame for this particular murder? Originally, when all of the other murders took place, he was not considered a suspect because of the fact that he was undergoing sentence. The catch comes in the form of the fact that, when McMahon was killed, Dupas was almost at the end of this particular sentence and was released from prison on an eight-day temporary release program in order to assess his suitability for release on parole.

The crime for which Dupas was serving a sentence was a violent rape of a 26-year-old female in a public toilet in Frankston. Frankston, Rye and Rosebud are all beachside suburbs outside Melbourne on the Mornington Peninsular and are in relatively close proximity. On his eight-day release Dupas was residing with his elderly parents in the Frankston area. He returned to prison, as per the conditions of his temporary release, on 14 February 1985, the day after the murder of Helen McMahon. Dupas was released from prison on parole a short time later, and was again residing with his parents in Frankston when he drove his car to the Blairgowrie back beach, not far from the Rye back beach, where, armed with a knife, he attacked and raped a twenty-one-year-old while she was on the beach.

What sort of supervision, if any, was Dupas under while he was on day leave? It would appear not much if he was able to travel to the beach and kill somebody, and to date get away with it.

While I was on day release from jail I was required to be at certain places at certain times and the jail rang and checked on me repeatedly. It seems they check drug users but not rapist/murderers.

As in the case of Halvagis and Kathleen Downes, no forensic evidence has come to light.

Renita Brunton

Renita Brunton died on 5 November 1993 at her store, Exclusive Pre-loved Clothing, at 3 Link Arcade, Sunbury, in regional Victoria. She was a strong-willed woman and set in her ways. She was apparently easygoing but not afraid to say what was on her mind. She made friends easily.

On the day of her death Ms Brunton was at her store in Sunbury, which was open for business. Several people had been in and out the store in the morning. The police have revealed that unusual noises were heard coming from the vicinity of Brunton's shop early that afternoon. While witnesses described the noises as "concerning", nobody investigated further at the time. Had anybody gone to investigate, chances are Renita Brunton would be alive today. Instead, the noises stopped and nothing else transpired for the remainder of the day – until about 5.30 pm when someone came to visit Brunton. The shop was still open, which was unusual at that time, and Renita Brunton's body was found in the back of the shop. Brunton had died as a result of multiple stab wounds to the chest.

At the time Peter Dupas was living in Woodend, close to Sunbury, with the woman to whom he was then married, Grace McConnell. On Fridays, where would Grace McConnell go to do her weekly shopping? Sunbury! On 5 November 1993, guess who went to Sunbury with Grace McConnell to do some shopping? Peter Dupas!

While Dupas has not been charged with this murder he is a suspect. If my involvement in the Halvagis matter is anything to go by, it is never too late to bring new evidence to light in such cases. Anybody who has any recollection of, or information about, anything relevant that took place or was noticed in Sunbury all those years ago, on 5 November 1993, they would be doing a community service to contact Crime Stoppers.

Kathleen Downes

Kathleen Downes was born on 29 January 1902, and on 31 December 1997, at nearly ninety-six years of age, she was murdered in the Brunswick Lodge Nursing Home. Mrs Downes has been described by staff at the Brunswick Lodge Nursing Home as a dear old lady with a wonderful nature. She was considered the matriarch of the nursing home.

On 30 December 1997, the residents had all gone to bed by approximately 8.00 pm. Staff always ensured that all external doors were locked and the premises were secure. In the early hours of the following morning, at about 12.30 am, staff made a routine check and confirmed that the residents in the eastern wing, including Kathleen Downes, were asleep.

At 6.20 am the same morning the day shift staff arrived and that was when one of the staff observed that the door leading into Mrs Downes's room was ajar. As she pushed it open she found to her dismay the bloodied body of dear old Mrs Downes on the floor. At the time of this murder Dupas had just moved from a flat in Rose Street, Brunswick, close to the nursing home, to a house in Cone Street, Pascoe Vale.

The Homicide Squad have now made a direct link between Dupas and the nursing home. That link is phone calls made from Dupas's phone in the weeks preceding Mrs Downes's murder.

More important, and far more explicit than the phone conversations, is Dupas's conversation with me in prison and his astounding voluntary admissions against his interest, which you can see in my statement. There I mention having talked to Dupas about the significance of the DNA evidence on the glove at the scene of the Maher murder, to which Dupas replied that he had not left any "forensics at Fawkner", meaning Halvagis, nor, more significantly with "the old sheila down the road". I have absolutely no doubt that Dupas was admitting to me that he killed Margaret Downes and that he had left no forensic evidence at the scene. When one combines the phone calls with the admission to me, Dupas is, in my view, a certainty to have been the killer of Mrs Downes.

Once again, if anybody has any evidence at all they should contact Crime Stoppers.

Chapter 14

The Vexed Question of Capital Punishment

> *Men are naturally disposed to do wrong, in public and private matters, and increasingly severe penalties have failed to check this.*
>
> – DIODOTUS, SON OF EUCRATES, TO THE GREEK POLIS AT THE TIME OF THE PELOPONNESIAN WARS

The Peloponnesian wars took place approximately 2,500 years ago. Aren't we slow learners? We still haven't got it. Increasingly severe penalties, such as life imprisonment, are not a deterrent to people like Dupas who are predisposed to commit horrendous offences.

Whatever is governing the behaviour of such offenders – genetics, childhood experiences, conditioning, or whatever else – deterrence does not enter their thought processes. In

THE VEXED QUESTION OF CAPITAL PUNISHMENT

Peter Dupas's case, as has been seen from the catalogue of convicted and suspected crimes, it is obvious that jail has no impact whatsoever, save to say that each time he is released he promptly reoffends. All the evidence shows a similar modus operandi in all his offences, the only difference between offences being that with each murder the attack has become more violent and vicious.

Dupas sits and talks to ministers of religion who visit the units inside prisons. I wonder whether he ever confesses his crimes to a priest or minister and whether on his death bed he will finally make a dying admission about *all* his past crimes. This man is so bereft of humanity that I doubt it.

This leads one to the question: Should capital punishment be reintroduced?

I have given this question a lot of thought in the five years while I was in prison. During that time, I was forced to live with people like Ray Edmonds, Peter Dupas and Leslie Camilleri, and three indisputable facts became clear to me from this contact.

One: These people, if released into society, would reoffend, and I say that without one moment's hesitation.

Two: Let's be practical. It costs you the reader, as an Australian taxpayer, somewhere in the vicinity of $75,000 a year to keep a man alive in prison. That does not include the medication they take all the time, or the around-the-clock maximum security. In total the cost would be more like $100,000 a year. On the basis of pure economic

223

rationalism, are we getting much bang for our buck? The answer is unequivocally no.

Three: These people have no chance of being rehabilitated. Apart from anything else, are we as a society prepared to take the risk that these people *may* be rehabilitated? A classic example is Peter Read, a notorious cop killer. Peter Read served well over twenty years and he was supposedly rehabilitated to the degree that he was able to practice as a draftsman in jail, readying him for release. Much to the disgust of the Victoria Police (with some justification, I hasten to add), Read had not been on parole long when he committed a number of serious armed robbery offences. No, nobody was killed, but his willingness to again use a firearm to commit a serious offence was indicative of the fact that it would only have been a matter of time before Read would have killed again if he had not been apprehended.

In my case the only way I overcame my drug problem was that I stopped using, and that was it. What rehabilitation did jail offer me? All I was offered was further medication! In other words, I had the chance to replace one drug with another – a one-way street to oblivion.

In any event, how do we ascertain that somebody is rehabilitated? Is it the sheer effluxion brought about by having to serve a very long term of imprisonment? Is it, like with Read, a matter of them indicating that they have equipped themselves adequately for the life awaiting them outside jail? Is it a result of intensive assessment by counsellors, psychiatrists and psychologists? If the latter, then this system is fundamentally flawed, because people like Dupas, Camilleri and Read are veterans of having been assessed and interviewed by such health professionals. They know the questions they are going to be asked, and they know precisely how to answer those questions so as to be seen in a most favourable light.

The problem with psychiatry and psychology is that it is all based on psychological assessments, and conclusions are all based on what you are told by the person you are assessing or interviewing. There are few, if any, objective physical symptoms on which to base a diagnosis.

A mate of mine who has a psychiatric qualification is of the opinion that, if psychiatry is all smoke and mirrors, where does that leave the practice of psychology? It logically follows that if somebody knows the ropes, and is devious, as most of these blokes are, then you will get the answer that will require you to give the go ahead to release the prisoner on parole. Unfortunately, the proof of the pudding as to the honesty of those answers, is well and truly in the eating, and no amount of speculation or guesswork by a health professional can change that.

Take, for instance, Paul Haig, who has recently made an application for a minimum term to be fixed by the Supreme Court in Victoria. Haig is serving life with no minimum for a number of murders. I served time with Paul Haig. He is mad, dangerous and has a very short fuse. If he were ever released into the community he is sure to wreak havoc. He is still at Port Phillip, not in protection, but in a unit where the better behaved prisoners are put. Everybody tiptoes around Haig like they are walking on eggshells, and that's because he is likely to go off at the drop of a hat. The worst of Haig's murders was when he shot a mother in front of her child – I think the boy was about ten years of age – a life-shattering experience by any account, but this child didn't have to worry about that, because Haig then comforted the boy before murdering him as well. His reason for murdering the child was that the child could potentially identify him. Anybody who is prepared to murder a child in cold blood like that, has in my view, forfeited the right not only to live in our society but to live at all.

The next contentious aspect of this is what categories of offences should carry capital punishment. In my view the first and most obvious category that should *not* carry capital punishment, and probably the one that elicits more hysterical and uninformed opinions than any other (both for and against), is that of drug offences. And no, this is not because I was a drug offender. I hold this view because prohibition never has worked and never will work. Like it or not, the drug war is lost, and it was lost before it even started. Drugs are here to stay. What are you going to do? Swing every second person in Victoria? I don't think so. Drugs are a health issue, and must be treated as such. If drugs were treated as a health issue, the constant squawking by politicians, police and other do-gooders that the police are undermanned would stop overnight.

At the time of writing this book the biggest ecstasy haul in the world took place in Australia. The electronic and print media were awash with customs agents and coppers, even the Customs Minister, all grinning like Cheshire cats at this momentous achievement. What precisely was achieved? Within days of this blow to the forces of darkness, drug experts and social workers were saying the bust had made no difference to availability on the streets or cost. The resources wasted and the corruption generated by police trying to enforce unenforceable drug laws make the whole thing absurd.

I call on the law makers in the parliaments and courts to look at this issue in a clear, cold, calculating manner and draw the inescapable conclusion: drugs are health issues and need to be properly addressed. We need to concentrate on proper education for the children coming through, and on rehabilitation and ongoing treatment, not jail, for those that will inevitably fall through the cracks.

I spoke recently about the issue of capital punishment with Peter Farris QC, a controversial Melbourne barrister, Peter's view was that four categories of offences should attract the death penalty. They are: terrorists, cop killers, rapist/murderers and paedophile/murderers. I would add another category: child murderers such as Paul Haig.

If convicted after due process, those people have, in my view, forfeited their right to live and ought to be executed.

The view opposing capital punishment is that nobody in our society has the right to take the life of another. But the recidivist murderers that I am suggesting ought to be eliminated have no thought for the life of their innocent victim. Now, this argument is as old as the hills. The bible says we should turn the other cheek, but it also says "an eye for an eye". So whichever way you want to look at this argument, there are two sides, and both have pluses and minuses in their favour.

The opinion expressed here is my view, and my view alone, and I know that it will draw a lot of criticism.

This is a debate we must have. I think there is a huge groundswell of opinion in favour of the death penalty in extreme cases, but I also know that no government will have the guts to run a referendum for fear of getting the answer they don't want: Bring back the death penalty!

Chapter 16

In for a Penny, In for a Pound

The history of our race, and each individual's experience, are sown thick with evidences that a truth is not hard to kill and that a lie told well is immortal.

– MARK TWAIN, *ADVICE TO YOUTH*

The Western philosophy of life is to begin your life, establish yourself and then ascend in a steady graph of accomplishment and fulfilment until, as a successful person, you grow old and ultimately shuffle off this mortal coil. Such is our philosophy that we do not entertain the slings and arrows of failure or mediocrity. I prefer, after the journey I have taken, to view life more as the Hindus do: the wheel of life keeps turning, ever so slowly, and during our lifetimes we suffer all types of success and failure, for nothing is certain. You enjoy the highs and endure the low points of your time on Earth, and how you behave and what you achieve as a person dictates how you return when you are reincarnated.

While I do not believe in reincarnation I do believe that life inevitably delivers highs and lows, joy and sorrows, in varying proportions, and that nothing can be taken for granted. Failure is always an option and can hit without warning at any time.

I have enjoyed the highs that a successful career delivers, together with all the trappings by which our society measures that success. In equal measure I have endured the mightiest lows that life can dish out: I copped five years in the slammer! My fall from grace was swift and brutal, ending with me losing everything that I had worked all my life to achieve. All the trappings of success are gone. On the other hand, I feel I am blessed because for reasons that are not immediately apparent to me. I have been given another chance.

No more Mercedes-Benz, big house or penthouse at the snow. I have even been taken off the dole by the powers that be because I was earning too much! Meanwhile, as this book goes to print, the Australian Federal Police continue to "investigate" me, allegedly for "proceeds of crime", in that I had the temerity to write Court in the Middle about my experiences and criticise the establishment. The investigating officer, Mr Gleeson would be better served investigating the perjured evidence that was given at my committal proceedings and which no one wants to know about.

The logical conclusion of the investigation is that if, some time down the track, an order is made for me to come up with a proportion of the income lawfully derived from writing, I will be in a negative financial position in that I would not even have had the safety net of the unemployment benefit to fall back on. It was conceded by the Crown in my case that I made no money from the sale of a few grams of cocaine to Tim Watson-Munro and that my offending cost me literally everything. How long do the Crown intend to pursue me? Do they want me to be on the dole for the rest of my life or am I to be given an opportunity to publicly demonstrate my rehabilitation?

When the search warrant on my publishers was executed I rang Gleeson and asked why he did not merely ask me for a copy of the manuscript rather than indulge in all his grandstanding. His answer beggars belief. The reason Gleeson gave for not asking me for a copy was that he feared I would destroy the manuscript. Can you believe such logic? I had taken a year to write a book, for which I had been contracted. To suggest that I would then destroy the manuscript left me gobsmacked. I suppose I should not have been surprised; I have dealt with the Federal Police often over the years.

While on the topic of my conviction, I have not spoken to my co-accused, Andrea Mohr, since I scored from her the day before my arrest. Recently my publishers rang and asked how long it was since I had spoken to Andrea and I told them. Much to my surprise I was advised that an email from

Andrea was at their office. I ought attend; there was nothing to worry about. Needless to say, I hotfooted it to Hardie Grant for a look at this email. I was staggered to read that Andrea has written a book and it is being translated into English (her native language is German) for publication by Hardie Grant. The matter of greatest interest to me was Andrea's total exhoneration of me and my alleged criminal activities. I wonder if she addresses further questions of a large amount of cocaine being taken by corrupt police from a safe house at 33 Grey Street, St Kilda, and which subsequently disappeared without a trace. Ethical Standards of the Victoria Police supposedly investigated this complaint previously, to no avail.

The police involved in that disappearance were none other than Detective Senior Sergeant Wayne Strawhorn and his cohorts Detective Sergeant Malcolm Rozens and Senior Detective Steven Paton, all of whom have been jailed for corrupt activities. And still the newly formed Office of Police Integrity appears to have done nothing further to investigate this and other complaints against Strawhorn et al.

When I wrote of Strawhorn and his activities in *Court in the Middle*, it was not known to me that Strawhorn had an appeal on foot. The behaviour of Strawhorn's lawyer Paul Galbally and counsel Peter Morrisey was extraordinary to say the least, threatening all and sundry with dire consequences if the book was not withdrawn from circulation pronto (my publishers were not intimidated; CEO Sandy Grant knows the law in this regard). Strawhorn's appeal was subsequently dismissed by the Court of Criminal Appeal and I can once again write about his activities.

The Office of Police Integrity was established by the Victorian Government a couple of years ago to try to deal with the burgeoning police corruption in the state. It does not have the powers of a Royal Commission or a permanent Anti Corruption Commission as they exist in New South Wales and Queensland. I am able to say, from first-hand experience appearing for clients before both the New South Wales and Queensland bodies, that they are formidable indeed. The governing legislation is so tough and tight that you rarely have anywhere to go and the result is usually swift and devastating. This is what the voting public wants but the politicians will go to any lengths to avoid. Why? The answer is simple: if the lid is lifted on police corruption in Victoria, that corruption will be shown to be present even in the highest echelons of the state's force, present chief commissioner excluded.

Police who get wind that they are, or may be, in strife retire with their fat pensions or prevaricate to such a degree that any investigation is ultimately stymied.

As I write this last chapter, a classic example of disgraceful police and political behaviour reared its ugly head again in the form of the case of Corinna Horvath, a woman who was bashed by police in her own home in the outer Melbourne suburb of Somerville in March of 1996 – yes, twelve years ago. The police officers who used what the original trial judge described as "unnecessary and grossly excessive violence" have never been charged. The state government was able to say it was not responsible for the misconduct of police who 'miscarry in their discretion'. The result of this disaster is that Miss Horvath has no damages or closure. Her solicitor, who underwrote the case, could not refund the costs he received after the win in the first instance and was consequently suspended from practice.

What happened to the coppers? Nothing. Yes, that's right. Not a sausage! Three are still serving members and have suffered no sanctions whatsoever. This is about the greatest travesty I can imagine. What message does this send to the public?

I am pleased to say Miss Horvath has now taken this matter to the United Nations Human Rights Commission, where it is my bet she that will win hands-down. All parties in this state who have contributed in any way to this extraordinary travesty should hang their heads in shame. This, after all, is Australia, not Communist Russia!

My life continues to be more than interesting.

When word got out that I was writing *Court in the Middle* the reaction from certain quarters was interesting indeed. For instance, my former legal partner, Brian Rolfe, rang my publishers and threatened Sandy Grant that he would sue if I said anything uncomplimentary about him. I had no intention of writing, nor did I write, anything about Rolfe.

Since my release the question most often asked of me by males is about sex in jail. I have reported that I managed to avoid any such advance. Sex in jail is rife and the authorities still ignore it and refuse to issue condoms. Apparently it is better to allow prisoners to cross-infect each other with HIV, or more particularly hepatitis, than address the issue and offend the lunatic fringe by allowing condoms to be provided. This problem is real: address it!

I know that I have rattled on for quite a portion of both books about the total lack of rehabilitation in jail. I read in the *Sunday West Australian* a short while ago that there was no rehabilitation in jails in Western Australia and that the system was in danger of imploding. Then, on 12 August 2008, a politician by the name of Stephen Wade from South Australia exposed the fact that in that state there are approximately 136 sex offenders in custody and that only twenty of that number have access to offenders' programs. Therefore the overwhelming majority of sentenced sex offenders in South Australia are released at the conclusion of their sentences without any, or any proper, rehabilitation. Believe it or not, in the same week as the South Australian minister made his findings, a Queensland politician added to the call to action by stating that Aboriginal prisoners in that state were being released without proper rehabilitation, which caused them to reoffend almost immediately because they lacked the educational tools for them to make their way in society.

LUNATIC SOUP

On it goes in every state and territory of this wide brown land – no rehabilitation. The point of difference between Victoria and what appears to be a common theme in all the other states is the complete denial by Victoria that there is a problem. If you don't own up to the problem, then how the hell can you fix it? It is about time all concerned – the courts, the Parole Board, the Office of Corrections and the politicians – pulled their collective fingers out and addressed the inescapable: there is no rehabilitation in prisons in Victoria.

As I said, working my way back to a normal existence has been a very interesting exercise indeed. People I knew before the wheels fell off, while they may have been ambivalent then, now fall into two distinct camps. There is no grey area, their attitudes are black or white: they are for me or against me. I have always polarised opinion but never has the divide been so stark. Some people who would talk to me previously have walked past me almost on a daily basis since my release and totally ignored me or looked straight through me.

I had a very wide circle of friends before I went to jail but that circle shrank dramatically and quickly upon my being charged and it shrank even further once I went to jail. Those who stuck have stuck like glue, and they were one of the main reasons I was able to get through my sentence. Without the support of all those friends, I would not have survived. They have bent over backwards to do whatever they can to help me get back on my feet in every conceivable way. Some of the help has come from the most surprising and unexpected quarters. My heartfelt thanks to all those people – most of whom have been quite direct with me in insisting that I make no formal recognition of them, so I won't.

Giving evidence in the Halvagis case was easily the most challenging thing I have ever done but at the same time enormously satisfying: it meant that at least some good had come from my incarceration. When I finished giving my evidence Mersina Halvagis's brother again approached Victor Susman, my manager, and asked that the family's heartfelt thanks be extended to me. Their view – win, lose or draw – was that at least the family now had closure, they knew who had killed their daughter and sister and could draw a line under their awful ordeal. The jury verdict was almost secondary; they now knew for certain.

At the time of writing this book, the matter was still subject to appeal, and so I have still not spoken to the Halvagis family. I do wish them well and I hope that what I have done has given them some comfort, to at least know that their daughter's murderer has been brought to justice.

In this book I have spoken often of life's little parallels but none blew me away more than what a friend of the Halvagis family told me only a few days before I wrote this chapter.

Many years ago two families lived in rural Warracknabeal and two little girls played together. Over the intervening years both families moved from Warracknabeal and lost contact. All these years later, those same two families are now reunited in grief. The two little girls were Mersina Halvagis and Nicole Patterson! What must the odds be of these two young women both being murdered by the same person after not seeing each other for such a long time?

I have been doing quite a bit of talking to school groups about the dangers of drug use. I enjoy the interaction with the young people and I am constantly amazed at the grasp they have of the issues. I do like the way they're uninhibited and ask confronting and intelligent questions. I find each talk I give to be a most rewarding experience. Do not under estimate these kids; they are smart and articulate. My message to them is a simple one: be safe and be smart. If you preach and threaten you lose your audience, but reason with them and they listen.

Earlier this year I was invited to launch the Red Shield Appeal for the Salvation Army for Central and North Queensland. I flew to Rockhampton and addressed a completely different audience – all good, salt-of-the-earth country adults. I loved doing anything I could for the Salvos; after all, they were there for me when I needed a friendly hand. My late dad always had a soft spot for the Salvos. He always told me that when everyone else has walked away from you the Salvos will pick you up time after time and never question or preach; they are just there. God bless the Salvos.

My life continues to be a great adventure. All I have been through has left me taking nothing for granted. I maintain the good health that I was fortunate enough to recover in jail. My two teenage children spend a lot of time with me. I have met a delightful lady, which has made my life complete once more. We are all very happy and, more importantly, comfortable each with the other. Life is great.

Having written two books I am working on a television project that I hope will come off in the near future. You can see that, after the journey I embarked upon that fateful day when I snorted my first line of cocaine, I am now in a very good place and I hope that each and every one of you who reads this book will heed the lessons of my downfall and try as hard as you can to not let anything similar happen to you.

Everyone says that you can't beat the system. But perhaps, if you keep nipping at its heels for long enough, you may bring about some change.